BARBECUES

HAMLYN
new
COOKERY

BARBECUES

ANNIE NICHOLS

PHOTOGRAPHY BY JAMES MERRELL

First published in Great Britain in 1995
by Hamlyn
an imprint of Reed Consumer Books Limited
Michelin House, 81 Fulham Road, London SW3 6RB
and Auckland, Melbourne, Singapore and Toronto

ISBN 0 600 58336 8

A CIP catalogue record for this book is available from the
British Library

Produced by Mandarin Offset
Printed in Hong Kong

ACKNOWLEDGEMENTS

Art Director Jacqui Small
Designer Barbara Zuniga
Commissioning Editor Nicky Hill
Editors Jenni Fleetwood and Elsa Petersen-Schepelern
Production Controller Melanie Frantz
Photographer James Merrell
Home Economist Annie Nichols
Stylist Sylvie Jones

Many thanks to B & Q, who supplied all barbecue
equipment. Thanks also to Baton Rouge, Blacks Camping
and Leisure, Bombay Duck, The Chelsea Gardener,
David Mellor, Debenhams, The Diningroom Shop,
Estilo, General Trading Company, Hilary Lowe, Indigo,
Jerry's Home Store, Muji, Oggetti, Peepul Tree Trading,
Spode, Summerhill & Bishop and Verandah.

*This one's for my partner Dave, my very best friend, for his
unceasing love, support and sense of humour.*

AUTHOR'S ACKNOWLEDGEMENTS

To my assistants, Sam, Sheila, Lucy, Cara and Teresa for
their very hard work and unfailing enthusiasm. To my ever
faithful friend, Pina, for her constant moral support. To the
team who helped put this book together, including Sylvie
Jones, Emma Hardy, Jacqui Small, Barbara Zuniga, Nicola
Hill and Penny Stock, and especially to James Merrell for
his glorious photography, inspiring ideas and patience.

NOTES

Both metric and imperial measurements have been given
in all recipes. Use one set of measurements only and not a
mixture of both.

Standard level spoon measurements are used in all recipes.
1 tablespoon = one 15 ml spoon
1 teaspoon = one 5 ml spoon

Eggs should be size 3 and milk should be full fat unless
otherwise stated.

Fresh herbs should be used unless otherwise stated. If
unavailable use dried herbs as an alternative but halve
the quantities stated.

Cooking times are approximate. They have been estimated
using a charcoal-fired barbecue and will vary according to
the size and type of grill, weather conditions and the intensity of heat. How far food is from the fire and the amount of
food on the grill will also affect the overall cooking times.

Before using wooden skewers or string, soak them in water
for 30 minutes to avoid burning.

CONTENTS

INTRODUCTION

Given the slightest whiff of summer, a strange phenomenon occurs. Men who aren't normally trusted in the kitchen are seen wearing *Man About the House* aprons and paper chef's hats, and sallying forth, tongs in hand, to rule the barbecue!

Barbecuing is fun and food cooked outdoors always seems to taste better. There is nothing more delicious than succulent, juicy food with a golden, crunchy char-grilled crust, hot from the grill. Even with our unpredictable summers, barbecuing has become increasingly popular in recent years. It's a healthy, exciting way of cooking and the choice of accompaniments, marinades and sauces can make it as simple or as spectacular as you like.

Cooking over charcoal is, in fact, a very easy cooking method. Given good preparation and planning, it should be a relaxed and enjoyable event. Just follow a few simple ground rules and you'll have time to spend with your guests or – even better – get them to take part! Throw a brunch barbecue. Serve Buck's Fizz and hot barbecued toast or brioche, topped with smoked salmon and soured cream. Prepare delicious Flip-top Oysters and Mussels – raw oysters and mussels in their shells, placed on the hot grill. They will open within minutes – just flip off the lids and serve with melted butter, wedges of lime and lemon, and Champagne to wash it all down.

Organize a barbecue on a crisp autumn day after a long vigorous walk to work up an appetite. Serve mulled wine and nuts toasted on the grill, while you wait for game birds or venison to cook. Even on a chilly winter's day, wrap up warm and have a barbecue picnic. Serve hot soup from a flask while the barbecue is heating and throw on some quick-cooking food to feed the ravenous.

You will find scores of suggestions in this book for different marinades, sauces and accompaniments. That is just what they are, suggestions – so try your own experiments with some different combinations and have fun!

CHOOSING A BARBECUE

With the vast range of barbecues now on the market, the choice seems endless and very confusing. This need not be the case; you should just identify a few important points that are crucial to your needs.

Decide how often you are likely to use the barbecue and whether this warrants a large state-of-the-art machine. Do you often entertain on a large scale or just for your family or a few friends? Perhaps you like to set off for a spontaneous picnic, where a small portable barbecue would be the most suitable. These are the most important considerations when you come to choose your barbecue.

GAS BARBECUES

There are many gas barbecues on the market and their main advantage is that the heat is instant and usually easily controllable. As long as you have enough gas on hand, you won't have to worry about refuelling the dying embers of a wood-burning or charcoal grill. One disadvantage is that they can never provide that delicious, char-grilled flavour that you get with charcoal or wood.

THE KETTLE GRILL

This covered grill with a hinged lid is useful in windy weather, when the hood acts as a windbreak.

When the lid is closed it acts like an oven; the food is surrounded by heat reflected by the hood, and so the cooking process is much faster and you can cook large joints of meat. Aromatics such as herbs or wood chips will give delicious flavour to food cooked in this way.

The main disadvantage is that the grid is not usually adjustable, and you therefore cannot regulate the cooking temperature very easily.

THE BRAZIER

These popular, portable, open grills are usually free-standing with wheels or detachable legs, though there are more sophisticated models with hoods and wind shields. Choose a sturdy model with strong legs set at a convenient height – they are often set rather low, and this can be back-breaking if you're tall.

Look for one with air vents that can be easily opened and closed, and an adjustable grill rack with two or three variable heights, allowing you to vary the distance from the heat.

Other refinements include electric, battery or hand-powered rôtisseries for spit-roasting. Again it is important to choose a model where the spit can be adjusted to different heights.

HIBACHI

The Japanese word *hibachi* means 'fire box'. This cast-iron grill is one of the most popular barbecues because it is small, inexpensive and, though heavy, easily transportable and thus ideal for camping and picnics. Small versions are perfect for cooking a barbecue *à deux*, though larger sizes are also available.

BUILT-IN PERMANENT BARBECUES

Build your barbecue on a site a little away from the house (to avoid smoke-filled rooms) and protected from prevailing winds. Line the inside with fire bricks, set a metal container on the base to hold the fuel, and a grate underneath for ventilation and to catch the ashes. Set metal pegs, nails or bricks poking out at different heights to allow the cooking grid to be adjusted. Complete packs are now available from DIY stores and garden centres with everything you'll need to build your own barbecue.

THE IMPROVIZED BARBECUE

Given a little inspiration and a few tools, you can improvize the simplest of barbecues, either indoors in the hearth of your fireplace (but don't use charcoal indoors as this can be very dangerous), or outdoors by setting a metal grid over some bricks.

I have fond memories of a winter barbecue in Australia. My friend Gabi dug a hole in the sand on a windswept beach, then filled it with kindling and set a metal grid over the hole. We enjoyed freshly caught fish and hot potatoes cooked in the embers as we sat watching the waves crashing against the shore.

OTHERS

There are many other barbecues available, including little cast-iron or terracotta pots, and even disposable barbecues which last for about an hour, and are fine if you are cooking just a few small items.

FUELS

If your barbecue is electric or gas-fired, there is no need to worry about the benefits of charcoal versus wood, though you will find the use of aromatics will give extra flavour to your barbecued food.

CHARCOAL

There is a good deal of debate about which fuel is the best to use for cooking on the barbecue. Charcoal is certainly the most common and my preference is for lumpwood charcoal or good-quality briquettes (though not the ones with chemical fluids added), because they give a good, uniform, intense heat.

WOOD

Hardwood gives off a very pleasant aroma, and you could choose from grapevine, cherry, apple, olive, ash, oak and many more. You should avoid resinous softwoods. However, wood barbecues need constant supervision to achieve continuous heat. So, unless you are lucky enough to have a reliable supply of hardwood, you will be much more likely to cook with charcoal.

AROMATICS

When added to your fire, aromatics will give off a very pleasant aroma and impart a little of their flavour to the food – a joint cooked in a kettle grill with hickory smoke is absolutely delicious. Packs of wood chips are now available from most DIY stores, garden centres and even from large supermarkets. It is not absolutely essential, either, to pre-soak wood chips as they can be sprinkled straight on to the coals. However, if you soak them for 1-2 hours before cooking, they will last longer and give a stronger, more smoky flavour.

Place the wood chips on a sheet of aluminium foil or metal tray and set this directly on the coals beneath the food. A tin can be placed upside down over the food to give an even more intense smoky flavour.

Try adding a bunch of woody herbs to the fire, a little at a time. The aromas of dried fennel stalks, sage, rosemary, thyme or juniper are just wonderful. Dried herbs will burn very quickly and so are better added towards the end of cooking.

LIGHTING A BARBECUE
Line the base of your barbecue with heavy-duty foil. This will reflect the heat and also make it easier to clean up afterwards. First spread wood or charcoal 2.5-5 cm/1-2 inches deep over the base to check you have enough. Pile the fuel into a pyramid shape and push a fire-lighter into the centre – or alternatively place dry kindling and crumpled paper under the coals. Light with a match and leave to burn. After 30-40 minutes, when the flames have subsided and the charcoal is covered in a fine white ash, rake the coals evenly over the base; you are then ready to cook. Do not be tempted to begin cooking before this, or while there are any flames – you will just burn and blacken the food on the outside, leaving it raw on the inside.

COOKING ON A BARBECUE
To top up the barbecue as you cook, place extra coals around the outside to warm up, and then gradually rake them into the fire, a few at a time, as they start to burn. If you add cold charcoal to the fire it will lower the heat. To control the heat intensity, push the coals apart for a lower heat or pull them together for a more intense heat. Adjust the height of the grill rack; sear food close to the coals, then raise the rack to finish cooking. It is also possible to vary the heat by starting the food over the hottest part of the fire then moving it to a cooler area to finish cooking. Opening and closing the vents on your barbecue, if you have them, will also help to control the heat.

Cooking times are approximate. They have been estimated using a charcoal-fired barbecue and will vary greatly according to the size and type of grill, different weather conditions and the intensity of heat. How far food is from the fire and the amount of food on the grill will also affect the overall cooking times.

EQUIPMENT
Although not essential, these items will make for easier barbecuing.

LONG-HANDLED TONGS
Useful for turning food and taking it on and off the grill. Use a separate pair for the coals.

PREPARING BUTTERFLY PRAWNS
1 *Remove the heads. Cut along the back from the thickest part towards the tail.*

2 *Open out the prawn and remove the dark vein running down its back. Press out gently to form the butterfly shape*

3 *After marinating, thread the prawns on soaked wooden skewers, then grill on the barbecue for 5-6 minutes, turning once.*

COOKING IN BANANA LEAVES
1 Dip the leaves in boiling water, then drain and place the filling at one end.

LONG PRONGED FORK
Don't pierce food while it is cooking; this will remove precious juices and flavours and dry out the food. Use only towards the end of cooking to check if meat or poultry is cooked.

SKEWERS
For brochettes and kebabs – soak wooden skewers for 30 minutes before use to prevent burning.

DRIP TRAY
Heavy-duty foil or a metal freezer tray can be placed on the coals under the food to catch the juices for use in the finished sauce, or to baste the food. It will also prevent flare-ups caused by dripping fat.

BASTING BRUSH
For basting food and oiling the grill.

HINGED BASKETS
These are great for turning whole fish or any fragile items with ease.

2 Fold one corner of the leaf over the filling, then the other. Repeat to form a neat triangular parcel.

LONG MATCHES
Extra-long matches make fire-lighting easier and safer.

OVEN GLOVE, CLOTH OR APRON
To protect you and your clothes from heat and splashing fat.

RUBBER GLOVES
For handling black and messy coals when setting up the fire.

CHOPPING BOARD AND KNIFE
Keep handy for cutting up food.

ALUMINIUM FOIL
To wrap food before cooking, to keep it warm and to make a drip tray (see above).

BARBECUE TIPS
1 Make sure you have ample fuel.
2 Keep charcoal dry, as it won't burn well when damp.
3 Allow enough time to start the fire properly and the embers to form.

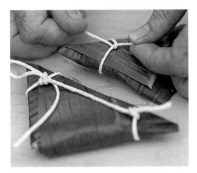

3 Tie a loop of string around one corner of the triangle, then the other. If you can't find banana leaves, use foil instead.

4 Always oil the barbecue grill well to prevent the food sticking.
5 Do not put salt in marinades for meat, as this draws out juices and dries out the meat. Season just before or just after cooking.
6 Keep food in the refrigerator before use, and then return it to room temperature just before cooking.
7 Cut food to an even size, so it will cook evenly. Place longer-cooking foods on the barbecue first, then add any quick-cooking items.
8 Remember food continues to cook after you remove it from the heat.
9 Sugary glazes should be brushed on just before the end of cooking – they will probably burn before.
10 Be well prepared, and keep everything you will need to hand.
11 Lean meat has a tendency to dry out, so bard it with extra fat or wrap it in bacon before barbecuing.
12 Never use petrol, paraffin or other flammable liquids when lighting your fire. Be safe!

FISH AND SEAFOOD

Whole Baked Fish in Banana Leaves

Measure the thickness of the fish; cook 10 minutes per 2.5 cm/1 inch.

1 whole fish, about 1.25-1.5 kg/2½-3 lb (e.g. parrot fish, snapper or red
sea bream), cleaned and scaled, with 2-3 diagonal slits cut in each side
1 tablespoon freshly squeezed lime juice mixed with 1 teaspoon salt
1 small onion, roughly chopped
1 red or yellow pepper, cored, deseeded and roughly chopped
2.5 cm/1 inch piece of fresh root ginger, peeled and roughly chopped
2 garlic cloves, roughly chopped
2 fresh red chillies, deseeded and roughly chopped
1 stick of lemon grass, chopped
125 ml/4 fl oz coconut milk
½ teaspoon chilli powder
15 g/½ oz fresh coriander
banana leaves (from ethnic markets) or foil, for wrapping

1 Rub the slits in the fish with the lime juice and salt and set it aside.
2 Place all the remaining ingredients except the wrapping into a liquidizer or
food processor and purée until smooth. Scrape the paste into a bowl.
3 Dip the banana leaves into boiling water. Drain and lay the fish on top.
Rub in a quarter of the paste, turn the fish over and rub in another quarter of
the mixture. Wrap the leaves securely around the fish, making sure there are
no holes; tie with string. Alternatively, wrap it in a double thickness of foil.
4 Place the wrapped fish on a barbecue grill over moderately hot coals.
Cook for 10-15 minutes on each side, until the flesh is tender. Transfer the
parcel to a large platter and turn back the leaves or foil to reveal the fish.
5 Heat the remaining paste in a small saucepan and serve with the fish.

Serves 4
Preparation time: 20 minutes
Cooking time: 20-30 minutes

Sole with Fruit, Flambéed with Pernod

Hot and cold fusions are one of my favourite food combinations. Sweet sole hot from the grill, with cool grapes and orange segments, is flambéed before serving. A delicious concoction.

250 g/8 oz black grapes
4 large oranges
4 lemon soles, about 500 g/1 lb
   each, cleaned and rinsed
butter or oil, for brushing
4 tablespoons Pernod or pastis
salt and pepper

1 Cut the grapes in half and remove the seeds. Place the grapes in a bowl. Using a zester or grater, remove the rind from 2 of the oranges and add to the bowl. Using a sharp knife, cut a thin slice off the top and bottom of each orange. Place 1 of the oranges, cut side down, on a board. Cut off the rind in strips, working from the top down. Take care not to remove any flesh, but remove all the pith. Hold each orange over the bowl to catch any juice and remove the segments, adding them to the grapes. Set the bowl aside.
2 Cut 3 diagonal incisions on either side of each fish, brush with butter or oil and season with salt and pepper.

3 Cook the fish directly on an oiled barbecue grill or in an oiled, hinged rack, over moderately hot coals for about 5-6 minutes, turning once, until just cooked.
4 Transfer each fish to a heatproof serving plate and divide the fruit and juice between them. Heat the Pernod in a soup ladle over the barbecue, pour 1 tablespoon over each portion and ignite with a long match. Serve the fish immediately. A salad of watercress and frisé would be a suitable accompaniment.

Serves 4
Preparation time: 20 minutes
Cooking time: 5-6 minutes

Swordfish with Fennel Seeds

This marinade reminds me of a wonderful holiday I spent on a Greek island – where I had deliciously fresh swordfish served to me straight from a wood-burning barbecue.

4 swordfish steaks, about
   200-250 g/7-8 oz each
2 teaspoons fennel seeds, crushed
finely grated rind and juice of 1 lemon
1 tablespoon bottled capers, drained
   and chopped
2 tablespoons chopped fresh dill
1 teaspoon paprika
1-2 garlic cloves, crushed
150 ml/¼ pint olive oil

1 Place the swordfish in a single layer in a shallow dish. Mix the remaining ingredients in a jug, pour over the steaks and toss to coat well. Cover and marinate for 2-3 hours, turning the fish several times.
2 Using tongs, remove the fish from the dish. Pour the marinade into a jug. Cook the steaks on an oiled barbecue grill over hot coals for 5-7 minutes on each side, basting frequently with the marinade. Serve with salad and plain rice.

Serves 4
Preparation time: 10 minutes,
plus 2-3 hours marinating time
Cooking time: 10-15 minutes

Seared Peppered Tuna

Tuna, lightly seared outside, rare inside, is served with homemade pickled ginger. Wasabi, hot Japanese horseradish paste from Asian food stores, may also be served. Some people are allergic to pink peppercorns, so you may wish to use crushed black or white peppercorns instead.

250 g/8 oz rice noodles
1½ tablespoons sesame oil
1½ tablespoons sesame seeds, toasted,
   plus 1 tablespoon, for garnish
   (optional)
2 tablespoons freshly squeezed
   lime juice
5 tablespoons groundnut oil
2 garlic cloves, crushed
4 tuna steaks, skinned, about
   175 g/6 oz each

4 tablespoons dried pink peppercorns,
   crushed (see introduction)
salt
PICKLED GINGER:
6 tablespoons rice vinegar
1 tablespoon sugar
1 teaspoon salt
50 g/2 oz piece of fresh root ginger,
   peeled and cut into wafer-thin slices

1 To prepare the pickled ginger, place the rice vinegar, sugar and salt in a small saucepan. Bring to the boil, add the sliced ginger, lower the heat and simmer for about 1-2 minutes. Remove from the heat, transfer to a bowl and leave to cool.
2 Prepare the noodles according to the packet instructions. Drain and refresh under cold water, then drain well again. Tip the noodles into a bowl, add the sesame oil and sesame seeds and toss lightly.
3 Combine the lime juice, groundnut oil, garlic and salt to taste in a shallow dish, large enough to hold all the tuna in a single layer. Add the fish, toss lightly until coated, cover the dish and marinate the tuna for 1 hour, turning once.
4 Place the peppercorns on a plate. Drain the tuna, discarding the marinade. Roll the edges of each tuna steak in the peppercorns to coat. Sprinkle with a little salt.
5 Cook on an oiled barbecue grill over moderately hot coals for 1 minute on each side to sear the edges. Slice thinly and serve with the ginger and noodles, sprinkled with sesame seeds, if liked.

Serves 4
Preparation time: 20 minutes, plus 1 hour marinating time
Cooking time: 2 minutes

Coconut Butterfly Prawns

A delicious starter, and a way of preparing prawns that is simple to do, looks good and also ensures even cooking – follow the step-by-step instructions illustrated on page 8.

12 large uncooked tiger prawns, in their shells
2 garlic cloves, crushed
1 cm/½ inch piece of fresh root ginger, peeled and very finely shredded
2 tablespoons freshly squeezed lime juice
1-2 red chillies, deseeded and finely chopped
150 ml/¼ pint coconut cream

1 To prepare the prawns, first remove the legs and cut off the heads with a small sharp knife. Holding a prawn with the back uppermost, slice along its length, from the thickest part towards the tail, cutting almost but not quite through. Carefully remove the dark vein that runs down its back.
2 Gently press the prawn to flatten it out and make the butterfly shape. Repeat with the remaining prawns and rinse well under running water. Pat the prawns dry on kitchen paper and place them in a large flat dish.
3 Mix the garlic, ginger, lime juice, chillies and coconut cream in a jug. Pour the mixture over the prawns, turning to coat them well. Cover the dish and marinate the prawns for 1-2 hours. Prepare 4 skewers and if using wooden skewers, soak them in cold water for about 30 minutes before use.
4 Drain the prawns and thread them on to the skewers as illustrated on page 8. Discard the spicy marinade, or retain and use for basting.
5 Cook the prawns on a well-oiled barbecue grill over moderately hot coals for 5-6 minutes, turning once, until the flesh is opaque and just cooked. Serve at once.

Serves 4
Preparation time: 10 minutes, plus 1-2 hours marinating time
Cooking time: 5-6 minutes

Stuffed Rainbow Trout with Soured Cream and Horseradish Sauce

Pretty, gleaming, iridescent trout are delicious with a simple lemony stuffing and creamy horseradish sauce.

150 g/5 oz butter
125 g/4 oz blanched almonds, toasted and chopped
125 g/4 oz fresh white breadcrumbs
finely grated rind and juice of 1 lemon
4 rainbow trout, about 375 g/12 oz each, cleaned
salt and pepper
SAUCE:
125 ml/4 fl oz soured cream
4 teaspoons grated horseradish
4 tablespoons chopped fresh parsley
2 tablespoons chopped fresh mint

1 To make the sauce, place the soured cream, horseradish, parsley and mint in a liquidizer or food processor. Blend until smooth, pour into a bowl and season to taste.
2 Melt 125 g/4 oz of the butter in a small saucepan, add the chopped almonds, breadcrumbs, salt and pepper, lemon rind and juice. Mix well, stuff into the trout cavities, then reshape the fish.
3 Brush 4 large double pieces of foil with the remaining butter, lay a trout on each and wrap up tightly. Cook on a barbecue grill over moderately hot coals for 20-25 minutes, or until the fish comes away from the bone, turning once. Serve immediately with the sauce and new potatoes cooked on the barbecue.

Serves 4
Preparation time: 20 minutes
Cooking time: 20-25 minutes

Seafood Brochettes with Saffron Mayonnaise

Monkfish and sweet scallops, lightly char-grilled outside and soft and tender inside, are served with a creamy golden mayonnaise. If using wooden skewers, soak them in cold water for 30 minutes before use.

375 g/12 oz monkfish fillet,
skinned and cut into
2.5 cm/1 inch cubes
12 scallops, cut in half crossways
into coin-shaped pieces, if large

MARINADE:
½ tablespoon freshly squeezed
lime juice

3 tablespoons sunflower oil
salt and pepper

SAFFRON MAYONNAISE:
pinch of saffron threads
1 tablespoon boiling water
2 egg yolks
1 tablespoon lemon juice
200 ml/7 fl oz sunflower oil

1 First prepare the saffron mayonnaise. Place the saffron threads in a small bowl. Pour over the boiling water and leave to infuse for 10 minutes. Combine the egg yolks and lemon juice in a separate bowl. Add the saffron and its soaking liquid and whisk the mixture until slightly thickened. Continue to whisk briskly, gradually adding the oil in a thin stream until the mixture forms a thick, creamy mayonnaise. Taste and adjust the seasoning.

2 Mix the marinade ingredients together in a jug. Place the cubes of monkfish and the prepared scallops in a shallow dish, then pour the marinade over the fish and set aside for 30-40 minutes in the refrigerator.

3 Using a slotted spoon, remove the fish from the marinade. Thread alternate pieces of fish and scallops on 8 skewers. Return the marinade to the clean jug.

4 Cook the brochettes on an oiled barbecue grill over moderately hot coals for about 3-4 minutes, turning frequently and basting with the remaining marinade. Serve immediately with the saffron mayonnaise.

Serves 4
Preparation time: 25 minutes, plus 30-40 minutes marinating time
Cooking time: 3-4 minutes

VARIATION

Grilled Lobster with Saffron Mayonnaise

Saffron mayonnaise is superb with grilled lobster. The lobsters must be killed immediately before grilling. The best method for this recipe is to pierce them quickly through the back of the head with a sharp knife.

2 small live lobsters
25 g/1 oz butter, melted
salt and pepper

1 Kill the lobsters as described above, then cut them both in half lengthways. Remove the head sac and the intestinal vein running along the top of the back.

2 Brush the lobster flesh with the melted butter and season with salt and pepper.

3 Place a drip tray on the embers of the barbecue. Place the 4 lobster halves on the grill above, shell side down. Cook for 3-4 minutes, then turn over and cook for 2-3 minutes more, until the flesh is firm and no longer translucent. Do not overcook.

4 Transfer to individual plates and serve with the saffron mayonnaise.

Grilled Tuna Niçoise

Seared tuna, served hot on a bed of robust Niçoise salad, makes an ideal barbecue lunch. If you can't find quails' eggs, use 4 hens' eggs instead, and boil them for 5-8 minutes.

12 quails' eggs
500 g/1 lb baby new potatoes
250 g/8 oz fine French beans,
   topped and tailed
4 tuna steaks, about 175 g/6 oz each
6 tablespoons olive oil
2 tablespoons chopped fresh parsley
½ tablespoon lemon juice
2 tablespoons mixed whole
   peppercorns, crushed
125 g/4 oz black olives, pitted
   if preferred
4 ripe tomatoes, quartered
12 canned anchovy fillets, drained
1 cos lettuce
DRESSING:
1 garlic clove, crushed
1 tablespoon white wine vinegar
5 tablespoons olive oil

1 Bring a small saucepan of water to the boil. Add the quails' eggs, then lower the heat and simmer for 3 minutes. Refresh under cold running water, then shell the eggs.
2 Boil the potatoes in lightly salted water for 10 minutes until just tender. Drain, refresh under cold running water and drain again.

3 Blanch the French beans in a separate saucepan of boiling water for 3-4 minutes. Tip into a colander, refresh under cold water and drain again. Place the quails' eggs and vegetables in separate bowls and set aside until required. Do not chill.
4 Place the tuna steaks in a single layer in a shallow dish. Mix the olive oil, chopped parsley, lemon juice and crushed peppercorns in a jug. Pour the mixture over the fish, turning to coat all the steaks. Marinate for about 30-60 minutes, turning once.
5 Using tongs, remove the tuna from the marinade. Pour the remaining marinade into the clean jug. Cook the tuna on an oiled barbecue grill

over hot coals for 3-4 minutes on each side, until just cooked, basting frequently with the marinade.
6 Meanwhile, mix the potatoes, beans, olives, tomatoes, anchovies and lettuce in a large bowl. Place the dressing ingredients in a screw-top jar, close the lid and shake until well mixed. Pour the dressing over the bowl of salad and toss lightly. Divide the salad between 4 plates and top each with a hot tuna steak. Serve with plenty of crusty bread.

Serves 4
Preparation time: 20 minutes,
plus 30-60 minutes marinating time
Cooking time: 6-8 minutes

Grilled Sardines with Chilli Oil

Homemade chilli oil – less potent than the commercial product – gives the sardines a slight zing without blowing the roof of your mouth off! If using the commercial variety instead, mix just a few drops with the 125 ml/4 fl oz of olive oil.

125 ml/4 fl oz olive oil
2 tablespoons chopped dried
  red chillies
12 small sardines, cleaned and scaled
coarse sea salt

1 Place the oil and chillies in a small saucepan. Heat very gently for about 10 minutes. Remove from the heat, cover and leave to cool and infuse for 8-12 hours or overnight.
2 Strain the oil through a sieve lined with muslin or a clean tea towel. Pour into a sterilized jar or bottle.
3 Brush the sardines with a little of the chilli oil, sprinkle with coarse sea salt and cook on an oiled barbecue grill over hot coals for 6-8 minutes, or until just cooked, turning once. Serve immediately, with lemon wedges, crusty bread and a tomato and onion salad, if liked.

Serves 4
Preparation time: 15 minutes, plus
8-12 hours infusing time (or overnight)
Cooking time: 6-8 minutes

Salmon and Samphire en Papillote

Samphire – or sea asparagus as it is also known – is a delicious coastal plant which grows on salt marshes. Here it is combined with rich salmon and a nutty pistachio and basil butter in a foil parcel. You probably won't need to add any salt as the samphire is already quite salty. Hasselback potatoes make the perfect accompaniment.

4 salmon fillets, about
    200 g/7 oz each
125-175 g/4-6 oz samphire

PISTACHIO AND BASIL BUTTER:
125 g/4 oz butter, slightly softened
50 g/2 oz unpeeled, unsalted
    pistachio nuts
2 tablespoons chopped fresh basil

1 garlic clove, crushed
1-2 teaspoons freshly squeezed
    lime juice
salt and pepper

HASSELBACK POTATOES:
16 small new potatoes
3 tablespoons olive oil
sea salt flakes

1 To make the pistachio and basil butter, place the butter, pistachios, basil, garlic and lime juice in a liquidizer or food processor. Add salt and pepper to taste and blend until the sauce is smooth and green. Spoon the mixture into a small bowl, cover and chill in the refrigerator.

2 Place each salmon fillet on a double piece of foil large enough to enclose it completely. Top each fillet with a quarter of the samphire and add a generous tablespoon of the pistachio and basil butter. Bring up the edges of the foil and press together to seal each parcel.

3 Divide the potatoes between 4 skewers. Using a small sharp knife, make thin slashes across each potato, then brush all the potatoes with the olive oil and sprinkle with some sea salt flakes.

4 Cook the potato skewers on an oiled, preheated barbecue grill over hot coals for 20-25 minutes, adding the salmon parcels for the final 15-20 minutes. Just before serving, carefully open one of the foil parcels and check that the fish is cooked through. It should flake easily when tested with the point of a knife, but still be moist. Serve the parcels on individual plates, with the Hasselback potatoes.

Serves 4
Preparation time: 10 minutes
Cooking time: 20-25 minutes

VARIATION

Ginger and Mint Butter

Use this fragrant gingery butter in place of the pistachio and basil butter.

125 g/4 oz butter, slightly softened
1 tablespoon grated fresh root ginger
2 tablespoons chopped fresh mint
salt and pepper

1 Beat all the ingredients together in a small bowl. Continue as in the main recipe.

Monkfish Grilled with Garlic and Rosemary

Rosemary is a very powerful herb which can easily dominate the flavour of the fish. Here the monkfish fillets are merely tied together with rosemary sprigs. so the aroma permeates the fish without being overwhelming.

500 g/1 lb ripe tomatoes, skinned
1 tablespoon balsamic vinegar
2 monkfish fillets, about
    375 g/12 oz each, skinned
4 garlic cloves, cut into thin slivers
2 long rosemary sprigs
5 tablespoons olive oil
1 tablespoon lemon juice
salt and pepper

1 Place the tomatoes in a liquidizer or food processor and purée until smooth. Strain through a sieve into a bowl, season to taste with the vinegar, salt and pepper, then cover and set aside.

2 Slice each fillet lengthways, almost but not quite all the way through, making a pocket. Lay the garlic slivers down the length of the pocket in each fillet and top with a rosemary sprig. Add salt and pepper to taste. Re-form both fillets and tie them with string at 1.5 cm/¾ inch intervals.

3 Mix the olive oil and lemon juice in a shallow dish, large enough to hold both fillets. Add the monkfish, spoon the oil and lemon juice over the top, then cover. Marinate for 1 hour, turning occasionally.

4 Drain the monkfish and cook on an oiled barbecue grill over moderately hot coals for 15-20 minutes, basting frequently, until the flesh is opaque and just cooked.

5 Remove the string. Slice both fillets thinly. Serve on individual plates, with the tomato sauce, warmed through, and good crusty bread.

Serves 4
Preparation time: 30 minutes,
plus 1 hour marinating time
Cooking time: 25-30 minutes

Cod with Black Beans and Ginger

Fish steaks, laced with Chinese black beans and fragrant ginger, then steamed in foil parcels, make an unusual barbecue dish. Fermented black beans, available from Oriental supermarkets, are a variety of soya bean that has been salted and fermented.

4 thick cod steaks, about
    175 g/6 oz each
1 red chilli, deseeded and
    finely chopped
1½ tablespoons fermented black beans,
    finely chopped
2.5 cm/1 inch piece of fresh root
    ginger, peeled and finely chopped
finely grated rind and juice of 1 lime
1-2 tablespoons light soy sauce
2 garlic cloves, crushed
2 tablespoons Shaosing rice wine or
    dry sherry
2 teaspoons sesame oil
2 spring onions, finely sliced
pepper

1 Place the fish in a single layer in a shallow dish. Mix the remaining ingredients in a bowl. Pour the mixture over the fish, turning to coat. Cover and marinate for 30 minutes.
2 Place each fish steak on a double square of foil. Turn up the edges of the foil slightly. Divide the marinade between the squares. Bring up the edges of the foil and press to seal.

3 Cook on the barbecue grill over hot coals for 10-15 minutes. Serve at once, in the foil parcels, with plain rice or egg noodles and steamed vegetables. Diners open their own parcels and mix the fragrant juices with the rice or egg noodles.

Serves 4
Preparation time: 15 minutes, plus 30 minutes marinating time
Cooking time: 10-15 minutes

Stuffed Baby Squid

Perfect for the barbecue, these sweet-tasting baby squid are filled with a Mediterranean-inspired stuffing. Make sure you do not over-fill them or they may split open during cooking. It will save time if you ask your fishmonger to prepare and clean the squid.

500 g/1 lb baby squid, prepared
   and cleaned
50 g/2 oz black olives, pitted
   and chopped
2 tablespoons bottled capers, drained
   and chopped
1-2 garlic cloves, crushed

4 tomatoes, skinned, deseeded
   and chopped
4 tablespoons chopped fresh oregano
125 g/4 oz fresh white breadcrumbs
1½ tablespoons lemon juice
4 tablespoons olive oil, plus extra
   for brushing

1 Chop the squid tentacles finely and place them in a bowl. Add the olives, capers, garlic, tomatoes, oregano, breadcrumbs, lemon juice and 4 tablespoons of olive oil. Mix well.
2 Use this mixture to stuff the squid. Secure the open end of each with a cocktail stick that has been soaked in water for 30 minutes. Brush the squid lightly with oil.
3 Cook the stuffed squid on an oiled barbecue grill over moderately hot coals for about 3-4 minutes, turning frequently, until just cooked. Serve at once.

Serves 4
Preparation time: 40 minutes
Cooking time: 3-4 minutes

VARIATION

Baby Squid with Chilli and Coriander Stuffing

Try the squid with this delicious South-east Asian stuffing.

500 g/1 lb baby squid, prepared
   and cleaned
3 spring onions, thinly sliced
2 garlic cloves, crushed
1-2 red chillies, deseeded and chopped
2 tablespoons chopped fresh coriander
1 lime
175 g/6 oz ground almonds
2 tablespoons groundnut oil

1 Chop the squid tentacles finely, place them in a bowl and add the spring onions, garlic, chillies and fresh coriander.
2 Grate the lime finely, then squeeze out the juice. Add the rind to the mixture, mix well and moisten with about 1 tablespoon of the juice.
3 Stir in the almonds and oil, and proceed as in the main recipe.

Grilled Mackerel with Plum Sauce

This pretty plum sauce is just perfect with mackerel, providing a slightly acidic counterpoint to the oiliness of the fish.

500 g/1 lb sharp red plums
25 g/1 oz sugar
1 teaspoon coriander seeds, crushed
1 garlic clove, crushed
pinch of paprika
1 teaspoon finely grated lemon rind
4 tablespoons water
4 whole mackerel, about
    375 g/12 oz each
salt and pepper

1 Cut the plums in half, remove the stones and cut the flesh into wedges. Place in a saucepan with the sugar, coriander seeds, garlic, paprika, lemon rind and measured water. Bring to the boil, cover, lower the heat and simmer gently for about 10 minutes, until softened.

2 Spoon the plum mixture into a liquidizer or food processor and purée until smooth. Sieve into a clean pan, bring to the boil and cook for 5 minutes, until thickened and reduced, stirring constantly to prevent the sauce from burning.

3 Cut 3 diagonal slashes on both sides of each fish. Season and cook on an oiled barbecue grill or in a hinged wire basket over hot coals for 6-7 minutes on each side.

4 Place the freshly grilled mackerel on individual plates. Pour the hot, thick plum sauce into a bowl or sauceboat, and serve immediately with the grilled fish.

Serves 4
Preparation time: 25 minutes
Cooking time: 10-15 minutes

Barbecued Squid and Prawns

When barbecued, the flavour of squid and the fresh prawns can be fully appreciated – this cooking method gives a smoky, sweet, char-grilled taste, a perfect complement to the hot peppery sauce.

375 g/12 oz prepared squid
12 uncooked king or tiger prawns, in their shells

RED PEPPER SAUCE:

2 red peppers
2 fresh red chillies
1 tablespoon sherry vinegar
salt and pepper

MARINADE:

3 tablespoons chopped fresh oregano
5 tablespoons olive oil
2 shallots, finely chopped
1 tablespoon lemon juice

1 To prepare the sauce, place the peppers and chillies under a hot, preheated grill. Cook the peppers for 10-15 minutes and the chillies for 5-6 minutes. Turn occasionally.
2 When their skins are well charred and blistered, transfer the chillies and peppers to a polythene bag, close the top lightly and set aside to cool.
3 Rub off the charred skin, then cut the peppers and chillies in half and remove and discard the seeds. Pat the vegetables dry with kitchen paper, then place them in a blender or food processor. Add the sherry vinegar and blend until smooth. Add salt and pepper to taste.
4 Cut the squid flesh into 2.5 cm/ 1 inch squares; score the squares in a crisscross pattern.
5 Place the squid and prawns in a shallow dish. Mix the marinade ingredients in a jug, then pour the mixture over the seafood. Toss to coat, then cover and marinate for about 30-40 minutes.
6 Using a slotted spoon, remove the seafood from the marinade, then pour the marinade into a jug. Thread the squid and prawns alternately on to wood or metal skewers. (If using wooden skewers, soak them in cold water for about 30 minutes before adding the seafood.)
7 Cook the brochettes on an oiled barbecue grill over moderately hot coals for 6-8 minutes, turning once and basting frequently with the remaining marinade. Place the brochettes in deep soup bowls and pour the sauce over.

Serves 4
Preparation time: 20 minutes, plus 30-40 minutes marinating time
Cooking time: 6-8 minutes

Cajun-style Cod

When making guacamole, be sure to include the flesh near the skin of the avocado – this is what provides the bright green colour.

4 garlic cloves, crushed
1 teaspoon salt
2 tablespoons chopped fresh oregano
2 tablespoons chopped fresh thyme
1 teaspoon whole cumin seeds
1-2 teaspoons chilli powder
4 green cardamom pods,
    seeds removed
12 whole allspice berries
2 teaspoons whole mixed peppercorns
2 teaspoons paprika
25 g/1 oz plain flour
125 g/4 oz butter, melted

4 cod fillets, 200-250 g/7-8 oz each
2 ripe plantains
juice of ½ lime
lime wedges, to serve

GUACAMOLE:

1 large ripe avocado
juice of 1 lime
1 large tomato, skinned, deseeded
    and chopped
1 tablespoon chopped coriander
1 small onion, finely chopped
salt and pepper

1 To make the guacamole, first cut the avocado in half and remove the stone. Scoop out the flesh into a liquidizer or food processor, add the lime juice and purée until smooth. Spoon the avocado mixture into a bowl and stir in the chopped tomato, coriander and onion. Add salt and pepper to taste. Cover the surface with clingfilm and set aside.
2 To make the spiced flour, place the garlic, salt and all the herbs and spices in a mortar. Grind with a pestle until smooth. Alternatively, use a coffee grinder kept specifically for spices. Tip the mixture into a shallow dish and stir in the flour.
3 Pour the melted butter into a second shallow dish. Dip the fish fillets into the melted butter, then dust with the spiced flour mixture. Place on an oiled barbecue grill over moderately hot coals. Cook for 2-3 minutes, turn over and cook for about 2-3 minutes more.
4 Meanwhile, cut the unpeeled plantains in half lengthways; brush with the lime juice. Place on the grill, skin side down. Cook for 2 minutes, until the skin is well blackened, then turn and grill for 1 minute more, or until the flesh is just cooked.
5 Serve the Cajun fish with the guacamole, grilled plantains and lime wedges. Add a crisp green salad if liked.

Serves 4
Preparation time: 25 minutes
Cooking time: 4-6 minutes

MEAT

Chorizo Kebabs
with Celeriac and Garlic Purée

Spicy Spanish sausages, crisply grilled and served with an unusual purée of celeriac and garlic. When garlic is roasted it loses some of its potency and imparts a rich, smoky flavour to the purée.

8 large garlic cloves, unpeeled
750 g/1½ lb celeriac, peeled and cut into 2.5 cm/1 inch cubes
25 g/1 oz butter
4 red onions, unpeeled
4 large chorizo or merguez sausages, cut into 2.5 cm/1 inch lengths
1 bunch of sage, leaves stripped from the stalks
salt and pepper

1 Place the garlic cloves on a baking sheet. Cook in a preheated oven at 180°C (350°F), Gas Mark 4, for about 10-15 minutes, until soft. When cool enough to handle, squeeze out the flesh into a large bowl.

2 Place the celeriac in a saucepan. Add cold water to cover and a little salt. Bring to the boil, cover, lower the heat and simmer for 15-20 minutes, until tender. Drain well and add to the garlic in the bowl. Add the butter and mash well, seasoning with pepper and adding a little more salt if required. Transfer the celeriac and garlic purée to a small saucepan.

3 Cut each onion into 8 wedges, cutting almost, but not all the way through, so they remain attached at the root end. Wrap in a double thickness of foil and place in the embers of the barbecue for 20 minutes, or until tender.

4 Meanwhile, thread the lengths of sausage on to 4 long metal skewers, alternating with sage leaves. Cook on an oiled barbecue grill over hot coals for 8-10 minutes, turning occasionally, until slightly crisp and heated through.

5 Warm the celeriac purée by placing it on the side of the barbecue grill, then serve with the baked onions and sausage kebabs.

Serves 4
Preparation time: 30 minutes
Cooking time: 20 minutes

Calves' Liver and Prosciutto Kebabs with Onion Relish

Succulent calves' liver wrapped in prosciutto is cooked on long skewers and served with a sweet onion relish. Wooden skewers should be soaked in cold water for 30 minutes before use.

375 g/12 oz calves' liver, sliced
  and skinned
6-8 slices of prosciutto
2 tablespoons fresh thyme leaves
16 bay leaves
2 tablespoons olive oil
salt and pepper
ONION RELISH:
50 g/2 oz butter
4 large red onions, sliced
2 tablespoons fresh thyme leaves
1 tablespoon red wine vinegar
1 tablespoon caster sugar

1 To make the onion relish, first melt the butter in a large frying pan. Stir in the onions and thyme and cover the pan. Cook the onions gently for 40 minutes, until softened but not coloured, stirring once. Remove the lid and stir in the vinegar and sugar, then increase the heat and boil rapidly to reduce the juices. Spoon into a bowl and serve warm or cold.
2 Cut the liver and prosciutto into 7 x 2.5 cm/3 x 1 inch strips. Place a strip of liver on top of a strip of prosciutto, then sprinkle with a little thyme and season with salt and pepper. Roll up from the short end and thread on to a skewer. Repeat with the remaining calves' liver and prosciutto until all the skewers have been filled, adding bay leaves at regular intervals. Brush the kebabs with the olive oil.
3 Cook the kebabs on an oiled barbecue grill over hot coals for about 5-6 minutes, turning frequently. Serve at once.

Serves 4
Preparation time: 1 hour
Cooking time: 5-6 minutes

Veal Escalopes with Artichoke Paste

These neat little parcels of veal and prosciutto are filled with a sweet artichoke and tomato paste, enclosing a soft, molten ball of mozzarella cheese. Bocconcini – miniature balls of mozzarella – are available from delicatessens and supermarkets, or you could substitute a whole mozzarella cut into four pieces. The veal escalopes should be very thin – place them between two sheets of polythene and pound lightly with a rolling pin, taking care not to make holes.

125 g/4 oz drained bottled artichokes in oil, 1 tablespoon oil reserved
4 sun-dried tomato halves in oil, drained
4 veal escalopes, about 125 g/4 oz each, pounded until thin
2 slices of prosciutto, cut in half
4 bocconcini or 1 mozzarella
salt and pepper
oil for brushing

1 Place the artichokes, the reserved oil and sun-dried tomatoes in a food processor or liquidizer and blend to a smooth paste. Scrape into a bowl and stir in salt and pepper to taste.
2 Spread each escalope with a quarter of the artichoke paste, top with a half slice of prosciutto and a bocconcini. Fold the veal over to make a neat parcel. Seal each end with a cocktail stick.
3 Brush the parcels with oil. Cook on an oiled grill over hot coals for about 4-5 minutes, turning frequently.

Serves 4
Preparation time: 15-20 minutes
Cooking time: 4-5 minutes

Kofta Kebabs

This speciality from the Middle East consists of spiced minced lamb or beef pressed around skewers, grilled and served with a minty yogurt dip. If using wooden skewers, soak them in cold water for about 30 minutes before use.

500 g/1 lb minced lamb or beef
1 onion, grated
50 g/2 oz pine nuts, roasted
   and chopped
1 tablespoon chopped fresh oregano
½ teaspoon ground cumin
½ teaspoon ground coriander
salt and pepper

YOGURT DIP:
350 ml/12 fl oz Greek yogurt
3 tomatoes, skinned, deseeded
   and chopped
1 tablespoon chopped fresh mint
pinch of cayenne pepper
salt

1 To make the dip, mix the yogurt, chopped tomatoes and mint in a bowl. Season with a pinch each of cayenne and salt. Cover the bowl and place in the refrigerator until required.
2 Place the minced lamb or beef in a food processor and mix to a smooth paste. Alternatively, pass through the finest blade of a mincer. Scrape into a bowl and stir in the onion, pine nuts, oregano and spices. Season with salt and pepper.
3 Mould the mixture around 4 long skewers, forming it either into sausage shapes or balls. Place the skewers on a well-oiled, preheated barbecue grill over hot coals and cook for about 10-12 minutes, turning frequently, until the meat is browned all over and cooked through.
4 Remove the kebabs from the skewers, if liked, or serve one skewer per person, together with the yogurt dip. Pitta bread and a crisp salad of cos lettuce are appropriate accompaniments.

Serves 4
Preparation time: 20 minutes
Cooking time: 10-12 minutes

VARIATION

Fresh Cucumber Relish

Try this as an alternative to the yogurt dip.

½ cucumber, peeled
3 spring onions, finely sliced
2 tablespoons chopped fresh mint
1 tablespoon red wine vinegar
grated rind and juice of ½ orange
salt and pepper

1 Peel the cucumber, cut it in half lengthways and remove the seeds, using a teaspoon. Cut the flesh into fine dice and place in a bowl. Add the spring onions, chopped mint, red wine vinegar and the grated orange rind and juice.
2 Mix well, add salt and pepper to taste, then cover the bowl and place in the refrigerator until required.

Stuffed Pork Fillet

75 g/3 oz ground almonds
4 large oranges
2 tablespoons clear honey
4 tablespoons olive oil
2 tablespoons chopped fresh oregano
500 g/1 lb pork fillet, trimmed
4 garlic cloves, thinly sliced
15 g/½ oz butter, diced
salt and pepper

1 Spread the ground almonds on a baking sheet. Cook in a preheated oven, 180°C (350°F), Gas Mark 4, for 10 minutes, until evenly golden. Remove from the oven, leave to cool, then place in a small bowl.
2 Finely grate the rind from 2 of the oranges and add to the almonds. Add the honey to make a paste, then season to taste. Peel and segment the oranges and set aside.

3 To make the marinade, squeeze the juice from the 2 remaining oranges into a jug. Stir in the olive oil and oregano.
4 Slice each pork fillet lengthways, almost but not all the way through, and open out like a book. Divide the almond mixture between the fillets. Drain the orange segments, adding any juice to the marinade. Divide the orange segments and garlic slivers between the pork fillets, arranging them on top of the almond mixture.
5 Bring the edges of the meat together and tie the fillets with string at 2.5 cm/1 inch intervals. Place in a shallow dish and pour over the marinade, turn to coat, cover and refrigerate for 8 hours or overnight.
6 Let the meat return to room temperature for about 1 hour then remove from the marinade. Season with salt and pepper and cook on an oiled grill over hot coals for 40-45 minutes, basting frequently with some of the marinade.
7 Transfer the meat to a platter, cover with tented foil and leave to rest while you prepare the sauce. Tip the remaining marinade into a small saucepan and boil rapidly until reduced by half. Slowly whisk in the butter and pour into a sauceboat.
8 Remove the string, slice the meat, and serve with the sauce.

Serves 4
Preparation time: 30 minutes, plus
8 hours marinating time (or overnight)
Cooking time: 40-45 minutes

Shish Kebab

Chunky pieces of juicy tender steak, marinated with onions, oregano and a zing of green peppercorns make marvellous kebabs when barbecued with yellow peppers. If using wooden skewers, soak them in cold water for about 30 minutes before use.

1-2 garlic cloves, crushed
2 onions, grated
finely grated rind and juice of
    1 lemon
75 ml/3 fl oz olive oil
2 teaspoons bottled green peppercorns,
    drained and crushed
2 tablespoons chopped fresh oregano
    or parsley
500 g/1 lb piece of steak
    (e.g. sirloin, rump or fillet),
    cut into 2.5 cm/1 inch cubes
1 yellow pepper, cored, deseeded and
    cut into 2.5 cm/1 inch squares
salt

1 Combine the garlic, grated onions, lemon rind and juice, olive oil, peppercorns and oregano or parsley in a large bowl. Mix well. Add the beef cubes and toss to coat. Cover the bowl and marinate the beef for 2-3 hours.

2 Using a slotted spoon, remove the beef cubes from the marinade. Thread the cubes on to 4 long skewers, alternating with squares of the yellow pepper. Pour the remaining marinade into a jug.

3 Place the kebabs on to an oiled barbecue grill over hot coals and cook for 3-4 minutes on each side, basting frequently with the remaining marinade. Serve shish kebabs with grilled aubergines and couscous, bulgar wheat or rice.

Serves 4
Preparation time: 10 minutes,
plus 2-3 hours marinating time
Cooking time: 6-8 minutes

Italian Sausages with Stuffed Mushrooms and Polenta

Tender mushrooms stuffed with creamy blue cheese are the perfect accompaniment to hearty Italian sausages. Add crisp golden polenta and you have a memorable meal. Grill the sausages slowly until browned all over, ensuring they are cooked through.

8 large chestnut or medium field
mushrooms
8 sun-dried tomato halves in oil,
drained and chopped, with
4 tablespoons oil reserved
250 g/8 oz Gorgonzola cheese,
crumbled
50 g/2 oz pine nuts, toasted

8 Italian sausages or other
good-quality sausages
salt and pepper
POLENTA:
750 ml/1¼ pints water
1 teaspoon salt
250 g/8 oz polenta (corn meal)
2 tablespoons olive oil

1 To make the polenta, bring the measured water and salt to the boil in a large saucepan. Reduce the heat slightly, and add the polenta in a thin stream, beating all the time. Cook, stirring constantly, for 20-30 minutes, until the mixture comes away from the sides of the pan. Tip the polenta on to a board or baking sheet. Leave to cool. Cut into thick slices, brush with olive oil and set aside.
2 To prepare the mushrooms, remove the stalks and brush the caps all over with the reserved oil from the tomatoes. Finely chop the stalks and place in a bowl with the chopped sun-dried tomatoes, Gorgonzola, and pine nuts. Add salt and pepper to taste and mix to combine. Use this mixture to stuff the mushroom caps.
3 Place 2 stuffed mushrooms on to a piece of foil large enough to enclose them, bring up the edges and seal well. Repeat with the remaining mushrooms.
4 Place the sausages, polenta slices and mushroom parcels on an oiled grill over hot coals for 15-20 minutes, or until the sausages are cooked, the mushrooms are tender and the polenta is lightly crispy on the outside. Serve at once.

Serves 4
Preparation time: 45 minutes
Cooking time: 15-20 minutes

Pork Chops with Gingered Apple and Rosemary Sauce and Grilled Parsnips

Pork and apple sauce are traditional partners. Here is a subtle enhancement, perfumed with fragrant ginger and rosemary. Grilled parsnips add a touch of sweetness.

4 apples, peeled
the leaves from 1 sprig of rosemary, finely chopped
2 tablespoons clear honey
½ tablespoon grated fresh root ginger
2 tablespoons water
4 pork chump chops, about 300-375 g/10-12 oz each
1 garlic clove, crushed
3 tablespoons olive oil
1 tablespoon sherry vinegar
500 g/1 lb young parsnips
25 g/1 oz butter, melted
sea salt and pepper

1 Slice each apple into 8 wedges and place in a saucepan with the rosemary, honey, ginger and measured water. Cover and bring to the boil, then lower the heat and simmer for 10-12 minutes, until the apples are tender. Leave the apple wedges whole or purée in a blender or food processor until smooth.

2 Place the chops in a single layer in a shallow dish. Mix the garlic, olive oil and vinegar in a jug, pour over the chops and turn to coat. Cover and leave to marinate for 1-2 hours.
3 Peel the parsnips and cut them in half lengthways. Brush them with the melted butter and sprinkle with sea salt. Cook on an oiled barbecue grill over hot coals for 20-25 minutes, turning occasionally.
4 When the parsnips have been cooking for about 10 minutes, drain the chops, reserving the marinade, and add them to the barbecue grill. Cook for 6-7 minutes each side, basting frequently with the marinade.
5 Serve with the grilled parsnips, the gingered apple and rosemary sauce. Grilled asparagus also makes a delicious accompaniment.

Serves 4
Preparation time: 20 minutes, plus 1-2 hours marinating time
Cooking time: 20-25 minutes

Lamb Noisettes with Mint Pesto or Aubergine and Olive Paste

Two delicious pastes, perfect with hot, freshly-grilled lamb.

8 lamb noisettes
2 tablespoon olive oil
salt and pepper

AUBERGINE AND OLIVE PASTE:

1 large aubergine, about 250 g/8 oz
125 g/4 oz pitted black olives
25 g/1 oz fresh parsley
1 tablespoon coarsegrain mustard
2 garlic cloves, crushed
salt and pepper

MINT PESTO:

25 g/1 oz fresh mint leaves
15 g/½ oz fresh flat leaf parsley
25 g/1 oz pistachio nuts, shelled
2 garlic cloves
125 g/4 fl oz olive oil
25 g/1 oz grated Parmesan cheese
salt and pepper

1 To make the aubergine and olive paste, place the whole aubergine under a preheated grill for about 20 minutes, turning occasionally, until the skin is well charred and the flesh softened. Cool slightly, slit the skin and squeeze the aubergine over the sink to remove the bitter juices.
2 Cut in half and scoop the flesh into a liquidizer or food processor. Add the olives, parsley, mustard, garlic and seasoning. Purée until smooth, spoon into a bowl and set aside.
3 To make the mint pesto, place the mint, parsley, pistachios and garlic in a liquidizer or food processor and process until finely chopped. With the motor running, gradually add the olive oil in a thin steady stream until amalgamated. Pour the pesto into a bowl, stir in the grated Parmesan and add salt and pepper to taste.

4 Brush the noisettes with olive oil, sprinkle with pepper and cook on an oiled barbecue grill over hot coals for 4-5 minutes on each side.
5 Place on individual plates, spoon over the pesto or paste and serve. Grilled courgettes and their flowers are suitable accompaniments.

Serves 4
Preparation time: 30 minutes
Cooking time: 8-10 minutes

Balsamic Steaks

Rich, dark, Italian balsamic vinegar is used in a marinade for barbecued fillet steaks. The mashed potatoes are flavoured with basil oil.

4 fillet steaks, about 200-250 g/
   7-8 oz each
2 red onions, sliced thinly into rings
3 tablespoons balsamic vinegar
50 ml/2 fl oz red wine
140 ml/4½ fl oz olive oil

1-2 garlic cloves, crushed
50 g/2 oz fresh basil, leaves stripped
   from the stalks
1 kg/2 lb potatoes, cut into large
   chunks
salt and pepper

1 Place the steaks in a shallow dish, large enough to hold them in a single layer. Sprinkle the red onion rings over the top. Mix the balsamic vinegar in a jug with the red wine and 2 tablespoons of the olive oil. Add the garlic and pour over the steaks. Turn to coat, cover the dish and marinate for 1-1½ hours, turning once.
2 Place the basil leaves in a liquidizer or food processor with the remaining olive oil. Process until smooth, then pour into a bowl and set aside.
3 Cook the potatoes in lightly salted water for 15-20 minutes, until tender. Drain well, return to the clean pan and place over the heat for a few minutes to drive off any excess moisture. Shake the pan frequently to prevent burning. Mash the potatoes in the pan while still warm. Stir in the basil oil and season with a little salt and plenty of pepper. Cover with foil and a snug-fitting lid to keep warm.
4 Using tongs, remove the meat from the dish. Place it on a platter, cover and set aside. Tip the marinade, including the onions, into a saucepan. Bring to the boil, then reduce the heat and simmer until it is reduced by about half. Place the pan on the side of the barbecue to keep warm while you cook the steaks.
5 Cook the steaks on an oiled barbecue grill over hot coals for 2-3 minutes on each side for rare, up to 4-5 minutes each side for medium (see cooking times, below). Spoon over the sauce and serve with the basil-flavoured mashed potatoes and a tomato salad scattered with chopped spring onions.

Serves 4
Preparation time: 30-35 minutes, plus 1-1½ hours marinating time
Cooking times: 4-6 minutes   (very rare)
                6-8 minutes   (rare)
                8-10 minutes   (medium rare)

The Great Steak Sandwich

This sandwich, spread with a sweet onion purée and topped with succulent steak, creamy fontina cheese, tomato and peppery rocket, is hard to beat.

6 tablespoons olive oil
2 teaspoons mustard seeds
2 large red onions, thinly sliced
2 garlic cloves, crushed
15 g/½ oz fresh flat leaf
    parsley, chopped
1 tablespoon balsamic vinegar
2 rump or sirloin steaks, about
    250 g/8 oz each
8 slices of olive bread or crusty bread
75 g/3 oz fontina cheese,
    thinly sliced
2 ripe beefsteak tomatoes, sliced
125 g/4 oz rocket
sea salt flakes and crushed
    black peppercorns

1 Heat 4 tablespoons of the olive oil in a medium frying pan, add the mustard seeds, cover and let them pop for 30 seconds over moderate heat – do not let them burn. Add the onions and garlic, cover and cook over a very low heat for 30 minutes until very soft but not coloured.
2 Purée the softened onion mixture in a liquidizer or food processor, then spoon into a bowl. Stir in the parsley and vinegar, with salt and pepper to taste. Cover and set aside.

3 Brush the steaks with a little of the remaining oil. Season with crushed black peppercorns. Cook on an oiled barbecue grill over hot coals for 2-3 minutes on each side for very rare, up to 5-6 minutes each side for medium (see cooking times, right).
4 Toast the bread slices on both sides until lightly golden. Spread with the onion purée. Slice the steaks thinly and divide between 4 of the bread slices. Top with the fontina, tomato slices and rocket. Season

with the black pepper and sea salt flakes, top with the remaining bread slices and serve at once.

Serves 4
Preparation time: 35 minutes
Cooking times:

4-6 minutes	(very rare)
6-8 minutes	(rare)
8-10 minutes	(medium rare)
10-12 minutes	(medium)

Grilled Kidney and Bacon Brochettes

The pancetta will help baste the kidneys and prevent them from drying out, while the sage gives the meat a delicious flavour.

500 g/1 lb lambs' kidneys
6 slices of pancetta or rindless streaky
bacon rashers, cut in half
1 red onion, cut into wedges with root
intact so the layers remain together
1 bunch of sage, leaves stripped
from the stalks
50 g/2 oz butter, melted
salt and pepper

1 Split the kidneys in half and carefully remove the core and fat. Score the rounded side of each kidney in a crisscross pattern.
2 Wrap a slice of pancetta around each kidney.
3 Thread the kidneys on to 4 long skewers, alternating with red onion wedges and sage leaves.
4 Season the brochettes with salt and pepper, brush with melted butter and cook on an oiled barbecue grill over hot coals for 3-4 minutes on each side, basting frequently with the remaining butter.

Serves 4
Preparation time: 20 minutes
Cooking time: 6-8 minutes

Butterflied Leg of Lamb with Flageolets

An easy way to barbecue a whole tender joint like lamb is to remove the bone and flatten it out so that it resembles a butterfly. This speeds up the cooking process. If boning and butterflying the lamb sounds too daunting, ask your butcher to prepare the meat for you.

250 g/8 oz dried flageolet beans
   or haricot beans
2 bay leaves
1 leg of lamb, boned and butterflied
3 tablespoons olive oil
4 whole bulbs of garlic
25 g/1 oz butter

1 large onion
6 celery sticks, cut into 1 cm /
   ½ inch pieces
25 g/1 oz fresh mint or parsley,
   finely chopped
salt and pepper

1 Place the beans in a bowl with cold water to cover. Soak overnight, then drain, rinse and drain again. Tip the beans into a large saucepan, add the bay leaves and cover with cold water. Bring to the boil, then boil rapidly for about 10 minutes, lower the heat and simmer gently for 50-60 minutes, until just tender. Drain the beans well, discarding the bay leaves. Set aside.
2 Remove most of the skin and fat from the lamb, leaving only a thin layer. Brush with the oil and place flat on an oiled barbecue grill over hot coals. Sear the meat for about 5-6 minutes on each side, then turn and cook for 10-15 minutes more on each side. About 8-10 minutes before the end of the cooking time, wrap each garlic bulb in a double thickness of foil and place in the embers of the fire to soften the flesh.
3 When the meat is cooked, transfer it to a platter, cover with a tent of foil and leave to rest for 10 minutes. Meanwhile, melt the butter in a large saucepan. Add the onion and celery and cook gently for 10-12 minutes, until softened but not coloured. Add the flageolet beans and heat through, stirring occasionally. Remove from the heat and toss with the mint or parsley.
4 Slice the lamb and serve with the beans. Add a bulb of roasted garlic to each portion and offer plenty of crusty bread.

Serves 6
Preparation time: 1¼ hours, plus overnight soaking
Cooking time: 40-50 minutes

Rosemary Potatoes

This is a delicious potato recipe to serve with fish, poultry or meat – especially lamb, which goes so well with rosemary.

4 long sprigs of rosemary
500 g/1 lb new potatoes, boiled in
   their skins for 10 minutes
1 tablespoon olive oil
1 tablespoon sea salt flakes

1 Thread the potatoes on to the rosemary sprigs, brush them with olive oil and sprinkle with sea salt.
2 Place on an oiled barbecue grill over hot coals and cook for about 10 minutes, turning occasionally.

Pork Kebabs with Prunes and Chestnuts

Prunes go marvellously well with pork. When marinated with the meat and then grilled they become deliciously soft and fudgy.

500 g/1 lb pork fillet, trimmed
24 pitted prunes
4 tablespoons Cognac
4 tablespoons olive oil
2 sprigs of rosemary, leaves stripped
  from the stalks, then chopped
24 chestnuts, roasted, dried or
  vacuum-packed
salt and pepper

1 Cut the pork into 1.5 cm/¾ inch pieces. Place in a bowl with the prunes. Mix the Cognac, olive oil and rosemary in a jug and pour over the meat. Toss to coat, cover and marinate overnight in the refrigerator. If using dried chestnuts, soak them in cold water overnight, then drain and treat as fresh.

2 Place the chestnuts in a small saucepan, cover with cold water, bring to the boil, lower the heat and simmer gently for 15-20 minutes, until just tender. Drain, rinse well in cold water and drain again.

3 Using a slotted spoon, remove the meat and prunes from the marinade. Thread on to skewers, alternating with the chestnuts (if the chestnuts are too soft to skewer, stuff one into each prune). Pour the marinade into a jug.

4 Cook the skewers on an oiled barbecue grill over hot coals for about 10-12 minutes, turning them frequently and basting with the marinade. Season and serve.

Serves 4
Preparation time: 15-25 minutes, plus 12 hours marinating time
Cooking time: 10-12 minutes

Marinated Veal Chops

4 veal loin chops, about 200-250 g/
7-8 oz each
finely grated rind and juice of
2 oranges
1-2 garlic cloves, crushed
3 tablespoons olive oil

WATERCRESS SAUCE:
150 ml/¼ pint vegetable or meat stock
1 bunch trimmed watercress, leaves
stripped from the stalks
50 ml/2 fl oz double cream
salt and pepper

BEETROOT CRISPS:
4 small whole raw beetroots, about
275- 300 g/9-10 oz each, peeled
vegetable oil for deep frying

1 Place the veal chops in a single layer in a shallow dish. Mix the orange rind and juice with the garlic and olive oil in a jug. Pour the mixture over the chops, turn them over to coat, then cover the dish and marinate the chops for 1-2 hours.

2 To prepare the watercress sauce, place the stock in a saucepan, bring to the boil, add the watercress and simmer for 1-2 minutes. Tip the contents of the pan into a liquidizer or food processor and blend until smooth. Pour into a small saucepan and set aside.

3 To prepare the beetroot crisps, slice into wafer-thin slices using a vegetable peeler, pat dry on kitchen paper and leave for 30 minutes. Heat the oil in a deep-fat fryer or deep pan to 190°C (375°F) and fry the beetroot slices in batches for 20-30 seconds, until crispy and curly. Drain well on kitchen paper.

4 Remove the veal chops from the marinade, drain and place on an oiled barbecue grill for 5-6 minutes on each side, basting often with the remaining marinade.

5 To serve, bring the watercress purée to the boil, stir in the cream and simmer for about 2 minutes. Serve the sauce with the veal chops and the beetroot crisps.

Serves 4
Preparation time: 30 minutes,
plus 1-2 hours marinating time
Cooking time: approximately
10-12 minutes

POULTRY AND GAME

Partridges with a Port and Grape Sauce

4 slices of pancetta or rindless streaky bacon rashers, cut in half lengthways

4 oven-ready partridges, about 375 g/12 oz each, stuffed with

1 small onion, quartered, and 4 strips of lemon rind

50 g/2 oz butter, slightly softened

1 tablespoon chopped fresh thyme

1 tablespoon chopped fresh parsley

4 tablespoons brandy, warmed in a ladle

salt and pepper

SAUCE:

6 juniper berries, crushed

50 ml/2 fl oz port

3 tablespoons redcurrant jelly

500 g/1 lb black grapes, cut in half lengthways and deseeded

1 Place 2 strips of pancetta across the breast of each partridge and tie with string. Mix the butter, herbs, salt and pepper, and spread over each bird.

2 Place a drip tray on the hot coals of a barbecue and place an oiled grill rack on the setting nearest the coals. Sear the birds for 2-3 minutes on each side. Raise the rack to a position 10-12 cm/4-5 inches from the coals. Cook the partridges for 12-15 minutes more, turning frequently, until the birds are tender and the juices run clear when the thickest part of the thigh is pierced.

3 Transfer the birds to a heated platter, ignite the ladle of warmed brandy and pour over. Make a tent of foil over the birds to keep hot.

4 Pour the juices from the drip tray into a saucepan. Add the juniper berries, port, redcurrant jelly and the grapes. Bring to the boil, reduce for 2-3 minutes, skim the surface, then pour the sauce into a bowl. Serve with the partridges. Grilled sliced potatoes and a watercress salad are suitable accompaniments.

Serves 4

Preparation time: 10 minutes

Cooking time: 15-20 minutes

Quail in Vine Leaves

Small birds are perfect for the barbecue and need very little preparation other than some protection to prevent them from drying out. Vine leaves are ideal for this purpose and also add a pleasant citrus tang to the meat.

4 large or 8 small vine leaves
4 long twists of orange rind
4 oven-ready quail
4 rashers of rindless streaky bacon
75 g/3 oz butter, melted
1 tablespoon chopped thyme leaves
8 slices of white bread
salt and pepper
FIG AND HONEY PURÉE:
15 g/½ oz butter
2 shallots, finely chopped
10 dried figs
2 tablespoons clear honey
50 ml/2 fl oz red wine
4 allspice berries, crushed
125 ml/4 fl oz chicken or game stock

1 To prepare the fig purée, melt the butter in a small saucepan, add the shallots and cook gently for about 5 minutes until softened but not coloured. Add the figs, honey, red wine, crushed allspice and stock and simmer gently for about 10 minutes. Remove from the heat, transfer to a liquidizer or food processor and purée until smooth. Transfer to a bowl and chill until required.

2 If using fresh vine leaves, remove any tough stalks, then blanch in a saucepan of boiling water for 1 minute. Drain, refresh under cold water, drain again and pat dry on kitchen paper. If using vine leaves in brine, rinse well in cold water, then drain and dry as above.

3 Wrap a piece of orange rind around each bird. Cut the bacon rashers in half and crisscross both pieces over each breast. Brush the quail with melted butter, sprinkle with the thyme, salt and pepper. Wrap the quail in the vine leaves and secure with string or cocktail sticks soaked in water for 30 minutes. Brush with any remaining butter.

4 Cook on an oiled barbecue grill over hot coals for 15-20 minutes, turning frequently.

5 Toast the bread until golden, spread with the fig and honey purée and serve the quail on top.

Serves 4
Preparation time: 30 minutes
Cooking time: 15-20 minutes

Turkey, Tomato and Tarragon Burgers

Richly seasoned turkey produces a mouthwatering burger.

8 sun-dried tomato halves in oil,
    drained and chopped
500 g/1 lb minced turkey
1 tablespoon chopped fresh tarragon
½ red onion, finely chopped
¼ teaspoon paprika
¼ teaspoon salt
4 slices of smoked pancetta or rindless
    streaky bacon, cut in half

TO SERVE:

4 ciabatta rolls
shredded radicchio and cos lettuce

1 Place the sun-dried tomatoes, turkey and tarragon in a liquidizer or food processor and purée until smooth. Spoon the mixture into a bowl and stir in the onion. Season with the paprika and salt. Mix well, divide into 4 and shape into burgers. Stretch 2 strips of pancetta over each burger and secure with cocktail sticks soaked in water for 30 minutes.
2 Cook on an oiled grill over hot coals for 20-25 minutes turning frequently. Serve at once in the ciabatta rolls with shredded lettuce.

Serves 4
Preparation time: 20 minutes
Cooking time: 20-25 minutes

Spatchcocked Poussins

Spatchcocking is a term used for splitting and flattening a bird for cooking. The method is ideal for barbecuing as it speeds up the cooking process and cooks the meat evenly. Here a sun-dried tomato and basil butter is inserted under the skin to baste the flesh while the chicken cooks and to keep it moist and succulent.

3 sun-dried tomatoes in oil, drained and chopped, with oil reserved	3 tablespoons roughly chopped fresh basil
125 g/4 oz butter, softened	4 poussins, about 500 g/1 lb each salt and pepper

1 Place the sun-dried tomatoes in a liquidizer or food processor, add the butter and basil, purée until smooth, then transfer to a bowl. Alternatively, chop the tomatoes and basil finely and beat with the butter in a bowl. Cover and chill.
2 Place each poussin breast side down on a board and, using poultry shears or strong kitchen scissors, cut down either side of the backbone and remove it. Turn over and open out the poussin, then flatten by pressing down hard on the breastbone with the heel of your hand.
3 Lift the skin covering the breast and gently push your fingers between the flesh and skin to create a pocket. Divide the butter equally between the poussins, pushing it underneath the skin.
4 Working with one bird at a time, thread a skewer through a drumstick, under the breastbone and through the second drumstick. Thread another skewer through the wings, catching the flap of skin underneath. (This will help to flatten the bird for even cooking.) If using wooden skewers, soak them in cold water for about 30 minutes before using.
5 Brush the poussins with the reserved oil from the tomatoes, place on an oiled barbecue grill over hot coals. Cook for 15-20 minutes, until the juices run clear when the thickest part of a thigh is pierced with a skewer. Grilled, sliced fennel and a chicory and frisé salad would be suitable accompaniments.

Serves 4
Preparation time: 25 minutes
Cooking time: 15-20 minutes

VARIATION

Tarragon and Lemon Butter

Use in place of the sun-dried tomato and basil butter. The quantity is sufficient for 4 poussins or 1 chicken.

125 g/4 oz butter, softened
3 tablespoons chopped fresh tarragon
2 shallots, very finely chopped
finely grated rind and juice of 1 lemon
salt and pepper

1 Beat all the ingredients together in a bowl or food processor and continue as for the sun-dried tomato and basil butter in the main recipe.

Chicken Yakitori

*These small tasty skewers –
the ultimate Japanese fast food –
are perfect appetizers to serve
with beer at a barbecue lunch
or dinner party. Small morsels
of chicken meat and chicken
livers are grilled until almost
tender, then dipped in a sweet
sticky glaze and returned to the
grill to finish cooking.*

250 g/8 oz chicken livers, trimmed
4 skinless chicken thighs
1 green pepper, cored, deseeded and
   cut into 1.5 cm/¾ inch squares
6 spring onions, cut into
   1.5 cm/¾ inch lengths
pepper

BASTING SAUCE:

4 tablespoons sake
4 tablespoons dark soy sauce
2 tablespoons light soy sauce
2 tablespoons sugar

1 Soak 16 short bamboo skewers in water for 30 minutes.

2 To make the basting sauce, place the sake, the soy sauces and the sugar in a small saucepan, bring to the boil, remove from the heat and set aside to cool.

3 Cut the livers into 1.5 cm/¾ inch pieces. Slice the chicken thighs into 5 cm x 1 cm/2 x ½ inch strips.

4 Drain the skewers. Thread the chicken meat on to 8 skewers and chicken livers on to the remaining 8, adding alternate pieces of green pepper and spring onion to both. Sprinkle with pepper.

5 Cook the skewers on an oiled barbecue grill over moderately hot coals for 3 minutes, then remove from the grill and brush well with the basting sauce. Return to the grill and continue to cook, basting frequently with the remaining sauce until tender. (The chicken thigh meat will take a total of 5-6 minutes and the chicken livers 4-5 minutes).

6 Serve immediately, with the traditional Japanese accompaniments of grated white radish (mouli) and sliced cucumber.

Serves 4
Preparation time: 30 minutes
Cooking time: 5-6 minutes

Duck Breasts with Caramelized Olives and Oranges

Salting the duck before cooking draws out any excess moisture and makes the skin crisp. The olives and oranges, cooked in an open packet, caramelize to a delicious, sweet accompaniment.

4 duck breasts, about 250 g/8 oz each
250 g/8 oz coarse sea salt
4 oranges
2 pieces of stem ginger in syrup,
   drained and chopped
125 g/4 oz black olives
15 g/½ oz butter
pepper

1 Place one duck breast, skin side up, on a large doubled piece of foil, sprinkle with half of the salt and top with a second duck breast, skin side down. Wrap tightly in foil. Repeat with the remaining pair of duck breasts. Chill both parcels for at least 12 hours, preferably 24-36 hours.
2 To prepare the caramelized mixture, finely grate the rind of 2 of the oranges, then peel and segment all 4, working over a bowl to catch any juices. Place the segments in the bowl and mix in the ginger and olives. Place this mixture on a large doubled piece of foil with the edges turned up (or use an aluminium tray), and dot with the butter. Place the open parcel on an oiled barbecue and grill over hot coals for about 25-30 minutes, tossing the mixture every now and then, until the oranges are slightly caramelized.
3 Meanwhile, separate the duck breasts, rinse them well and pat dry on kitchen paper. Cook on the oiled barbecue grill, skin side down for the first 5 minutes, then turn and seal the other side. Continue cooking the duck alongside the parcel of olives and oranges for 10-15 minutes, turning occasionally, until the duck skin is crisp and the flesh tender but still pink. Serve with the olive and orange mixture and a leafy salad.

Serves 4
Preparation time: 15 minutes, plus 12-36 hours to salt the duck
Cooking time: 25-30 minutes

Chicken and Herb Caillettes

These tasty smooth chicken burgers are wrapped in lacy caul fat. This not only bastes the meat and protects it from drying out but also gives the burgers added flavour. Caul fat is available from good butchers.

125 g/4 oz piece of day-old bread,
    crusts removed
300 ml/½ pint milk
500 g/1 lb skinless, boneless
    chicken, cubed
1 egg white
150 ml/¼ pint double cream
2 shallots, finely chopped
2 teaspoons chopped fresh parsley
2 teaspoons chopped fresh thyme

300 g/10 oz caul fat
8-12 sage leaves
salt and pepper

PEACH RELISH:
6 ripe peaches
2 tablespoons chopped red onion
1-2 green chillies, deseeded and
    chopped
½ tablespoon walnut oil
salt and pepper

1 Place the bread in a bowl, pour over the milk and leave to stand for about 10 minutes. Squeeze the bread, discarding the milk used for soaking, and place in a food processor. Add the chicken and process to a smooth textured paste. Alternatively, pass the chicken and bread through the fine blade of a mincer.
2 Spoon the mixture into a bowl and stir in the egg white, cream, shallots and chopped parsley and thyme. Season with salt and pepper.
3 Divide the mixture into 8 and shape into burgers. Soak the caul fat in warm water for 5 minutes, drain and stretch it out on a chopping board. Cut out eight 15 cm/6 inch squares. Place 1-2 sage leaves in the centre of each square and top with one of the chicken burgers. Fold the caul fat over and secure the back of the caillette with a cocktail stick. Make 7 more caillettes in the same way. Transfer to a baking sheet, cover and place in the refrigerator to chill and firm.
4 To make the relish, score a cross on the top of each peach. Plunge them into boiling water for 20 seconds, then transfer them to a bowl of cold water. Slip off the skins, cut in half and discard the stones. Chop them finely and place in a bowl with the onion, chillies and walnut oil. Mix well and season to taste.
5 Remove from the refrigerator 20-30 minutes before cooking. Cook on an oiled barbecue grill over moderately hot coals for 15-20 minutes, turning frequently. Serve with the peach relish.

Serves 4
Preparation time: 50 minutes
Cooking time: 15-20 minutes

VARIATION
Papaya Relish

1 small, ripe papaya
2 tablespoons chopped mild onion
    (red or white)
1-2 green chillies, deseeded and
    chopped
½ tablespoon walnut oil
salt and pepper

1 Peel the papaya and cut it in half lengthways. Scoop out the seeds, then cut the flesh into small cubes. Place in a bowl.
2 Add the onion, chillies, walnut oil and salt and pepper and proceed as in the main recipe.

Cinnamon-spiced Chicken Wings with Yellow Pepper Dip

Unusual, sweet and spicy.

8 large chicken wings
MARINADE:
1 garlic clove
5 cm/2 inch piece of fresh root ginger,
   peeled and chopped
juice and finely grated rind of
   2 limes or 1 lemon
2 tablespoons light soy sauce
2 tablespoons groundnut oil
2 teaspoons ground cinnamon
1 teaspoon ground turmeric
2 tablespoons honey
salt
YELLOW PEPPER DIP:
2 yellow peppers
4 tablespoons natural yogurt
1 tablespoon dark soy sauce
1 tablespoon chopped fresh
   coriander (optional)
pepper

1 Place all the marinade ingredients in a liquidizer or food processor and blend until very smooth.
2 Place the chicken in a bowl, pour over the marinade, toss, cover and leave to marinate for 1-2 hours.
3 To make the yellow pepper dip, place the yellow peppers under a preheated grill for about 10 minutes, turning until well charred and blistered. Place in a plastic bag until cool, then peel, deseed and place the flesh in a liquidizer or food processor with the yogurt and blend until smooth. Pour into a bowl, season with the soy sauce and pepper to taste, stir in the chopped coriander, if using, and set aside.

4 Drain the chicken and cook on a barbecue grill for 4-5 minutes each side, basting with the remaining marinade. Serve with the dip.

Serves 4
Preparation time: 30 minutes, plus 1-2 hours marinating time
Cooking time: 8-10 minutes

Chicken in a Green Almond Sauce

Delicious – chicken breasts covered with a paste of almonds and herbs and cooked in foil packages on top of the grill.

125 g/4 oz whole blanched almonds
2 garlic cloves, crushed
1 small onion, coarsely chopped
2 green chillies, deseeded and
    chopped (optional)
25 g/1 oz fresh coriander
25 g/1oz flat leaf parsley
6 tablespoons olive oil
4 boneless chicken breasts,
    about 175 g/6 oz each
salt and pepper

1 Place the almonds, garlic, onion, green chillies, if using, coriander, parsley and olive oil in a liquidizer or food processor and purée until smooth and green. Season to taste.
2 Place each chicken breast on a separate piece of foil and divide the almond sauce between them.
3 Bring up the edges of the foil and press together to seal. Place on a barbecue grill and cook over hot coals for 20-25 minutes, until tender. Serve with plain rice and barbecued red and yellow peppers.

Serves 4
Preparation time: 10 minutes
Cooking time: 20-25 minutes

Chicken Tikka Kebabs with Naan

Homemade naan bread is so delicious that it is well worth the effort of making it – especially when it is to be served with these spicy kebabs.

4 naan breads (see right)
750 g/1½ lb skinless, boneless
   chicken breasts, cut into
   2.5 cm/1 inch cubes
lemon or lime wedges, to garnish
MARINADE:
1 onion, roughly chopped
2.5 cm/1 inch piece of fresh root
   ginger, peeled and
   roughly chopped

2 garlic cloves, crushed
150 ml/¼ pint natural yogurt
1-2 red chillies, deseeded
   and chopped
2 teaspoons ground coriander
1 teaspoon ground cumin
½ teaspoon turmeric
juice of 1 lemon
1 teaspoon salt

1 Make the naan as described at right. Leave to cool, then wrap in foil.
2 To make the marinade, combine all ingredients in a liquidizer or food processor and purée until smooth.
3 Place the chicken cubes in a shallow bowl, pour over the marinade and toss well to coat. Cover the bowl and leave the chicken to marinate in the refrigerator for 8 hours or overnight.
4 Remove the chicken with a slotted spoon and pour the marinade into a jug.
5 If using wooden skewers, soak them in water for 30 minutes before using, then thread the chicken on to 8 skewers.
6 Cook the kebabs on an oiled barbecue grill over hot coals for 6 minutes on each side, basting frequently with the marinade.
7 While the kebabs are cooking, heat the parcels of naan bread on the edge of the barbecue grill.
8 Serve the kebabs with the naan and garnish with wedges of lemon or lime.

Serves 4
Preparation time: 30 minutes, plus 8 hours marinating time (or overnight)
Cooking time: 12-15 minutes

Naan Bread

1 teaspoon dried yeast
1 teaspoon sugar
50 ml/2 fl oz warm milk
250 g/8 oz plain flour
½ teaspoon salt
1 tablespoon vegetable oil
1 egg, beaten
4 tablespoons natural yogurt

1 Sprinkle the yeast and sugar over the milk. Mix, cover and keep warm for 15-20 minutes, until frothy.
2 Sift the flour and salt into a large bowl, make a well in the centre and add the rest of the ingredients, plus the yeast mixture. Mix, gradually incorporating the flour until the dough forms a soft ball. Turn out on to a floured work surface, knead for 10 minutes until smooth, then place in an oiled bowl. Cover and leave to rise in a warm place for 1 hour or until the dough has doubled in bulk.
3 Return to the floured surface, punch down to remove the air, then knead for 5 minutes. Divide into 4, roll into 20 x 12 cm/8 x 5 inch tear shapes, place on an oiled baking sheet, cover and leave to rise for 25 minutes in a warm place.
4 Heat a cast-iron pan, cook each piece of dough for 3 minutes, turn and place them under a grill for 2-3 minutes, until golden and spotty.

Serves 4
Preparation time: 2 hours 10 minutes
Cooking time: 12-15 minutes

Pink Pigeon Breast Salad

A pretty salad of warm pigeon breasts with pink peppercorns, pomegranate and raspberries – a stunning debut for a smart barbecue party. Some people are allergic to pink peppercorns, so you may wish to substitute crushed black or white ones.

1 pomegranate
2 shallots, chopped
1 teaspoon pink peppercorns, bottled
   in brine, drained and crushed
   (see introduction)
8 wood pigeon breasts
1 tablespoon sugar
125 g/4 oz raspberries, hulled
melted butter, for brushing
1 radicchio, separated into leaves
1 bunch of watercress or rocket
50 g/2 oz walnuts, chopped

1 Break open the pomegranate and remove the seeds, discarding the bitter yellow pith. Set aside a quarter of the seeds for the sauce and place the rest in a blender or food processor. Process just long enough to release the juice, then strain through a fine sieve into a shallow bowl. Add the shallots and pink peppercorns. Mix well, then add the pigeon breasts and toss to coat. Cover the dish and marinate for about 1-2 hours.

2 Using a slotted spoon, lift the pigeon breasts out of the marinade and set aside. Pour the marinade into a saucepan, stir in the sugar, bring to the boil and cook until reduced by half. Add the raspberries and reserved pomegranate seeds, remove from the heat immediately and set the sauce aside while you cook the pigeon breasts.

3 Brush the pigeon breasts with a little melted butter. Place on an oiled barbecue grill over hot coals and sear quickly on both sides for about 1-2 minutes. Remove the breasts from the heat and slice thinly.

4 Arrange the radicchio and watercress or rocket on 4 plates. Top with the pigeon breasts, spoon over the sauce and sprinkle with the chopped walnuts. Serve at once.

Serves 4 as a starter
Preparation time: 20 minutes, plus 1-2 hours marinating time
Cooking time: 4-6 minutes

Venison Cutlets with Red Juniper Pears

Pears in red wine, usually seen as a dessert, are also wonderful with rich venison.

4 firm dessert pears
2 tablespoons lemon juice
300 ml/½ pint red wine
6 juniper berries, crushed
pared rind of 1 lemon cut into
 fine julienne strips
1 stick of cinnamon
3 tablespoons redcurrant jelly
8 venison cutlets
oil or melted butter, for brushing

1 Peel the pears, then halve them lengthways and remove each core with a melon baller. Brush the flesh with the lemon juice to prevent the pears from discolouring.

2 Combine the wine, juniper berries, lemon rind and cinnamon stick in a saucepan. Bring to the boil, add the pears, cover and simmer gently for 10 minutes or until tender.

3 Using a slotted spoon, transfer the pears to a bowl and set aside. Stir the redcurrant jelly into the liquid remaining in the pan. Boil until reduced by half, pour over the pears and leave to cool.

4 Brush the venison cutlets with a little oil or butter. Cook on an oiled barbecue grill over hot coals for 2-3 minutes on each side. To serve, place 2 cutlets on each plate and add a portion of pears. Garnish with watercress and serve the remaining pears separately.

Serves 4
Preparation time: 20 minutes
Cooking time: 6-8 minutes

Guinea Fowl with Mushroom Stuffing

The guinea fowl are split open for ease of cooking and stuffed under the skin with a mushroom mixture which keeps the flesh moist during grilling. Serve with cidered or grilled apple rings (see right).

1-1.5 kg/2-3 lb guinea fowl
butter or oil, for brushing
MUSHROOM STUFFING:
25 g/1 oz dried porcini mushrooms,
    steeped for 30 minutes in warm
    water to cover
50 g/2 oz butter

2 shallots, finely chopped
1 garlic clove, crushed
250 g/8 oz field mushrooms,
    finely chopped
2 tablespoons chopped fresh parsley
salt and pepper

1 To make the stuffing, drain the mushrooms through a sieve lined with kitchen paper or a coffee filter paper. Reserve the liquid. Rinse the mushrooms under cold water, drain again, then chop finely.

2 Melt the butter in a saucepan. Add the shallots and garlic and cook gently for 2-3 minutes, until softened but not coloured. Add both types of mushrooms and cook for 4-5 minutes more. Stir in the reserved mushroom liquid and boil hard until all the liquid has evaporated. Off the heat, stir in the parsley and add salt and pepper to taste. Cool slightly.

3 Using poultry shears or strong kitchen scissors, cut the guinea fowl down either side of the backbone and remove it. Place the bird on a clean surface, breast upward. Press down firmly with the heel of your hand to break the breastbone and flatten the bird.

4 Lift and loosen the skin gently, easing it away from the breast and leg meat with your fingers. Take care not to make any holes. Spoon the stuffing under the skin and spread it out evenly. Pull the skin back tightly over the bird and secure underneath with a skewer or cocktail sticks.

5 Brush the guinea fowl with a little butter or oil. Cook breast side down on an oiled barbecue grill over hot coals for 10-15 minutes. Turn the bird over and cook for 10-15 minutes more. Continue cooking, turning occasionally, until the juices run clear when the thickest part of a thigh is pierced with a fork or skewer.

6 Transfer the guinea fowl to a platter, cover with tented foil and keep hot until ready to carve. Serve with the cidered apple rings.

Serves 4
Preparation time: 35 minutes, plus soaking time
Cooking time: 40-50 minutes

Cidered Apple Rings

25 g/1 oz butter
3 red dessert apples, cored and sliced
    into 5 mm/¼ inch rings
250 ml/8 fl oz dry cider
2 tablespoons Calvados (optional)
250 ml/8 fl oz crème fraîche
salt and pepper

1 Heat the butter in a large frying pan, add the apples and cook for 4-5 minutes, until golden. Using a slotted spoon, transfer the apple rings to a plate. Add the cider to the pan, raise the heat and cook until reduced by half. Stir in the Calvados and crème fraîche and cook for 3-4 minutes, until thickened. Add the apples to the pan and heat through.

Serves 4
Preparation time: 5 minutes
Cooking time: 10 minutes

VARIATION

Grilled Apple Rings

3 apples, cored and sliced into rings
25 g/1 oz butter, melted

1 Brush the apple rings with melted butter, place on an oiled grill over hot coals and cook for 2-3 minutes on each side.

Red Hot Turkey Focaccia Sandwich

4 x 125 g/4 oz turkey escalopes
4 tablespoons olive oil
3 tablespoons orange juice
1 large loaf of focaccia or olive bread
4 artichokes in oil, drained and sliced
1 red onion, thinly sliced into rings
125 g/4 oz rocket
salt and pepper

RED HOT MAYONNAISE:

2 red chillies
2 egg yolks
1 tablespoon white wine vinegar
200 ml/7 fl oz sunflower oil
2 garlic cloves, crushed
25 g/1 oz pine nuts
4 tablespoons grated Parmesan cheese
8 sun-dried tomato halves in oil

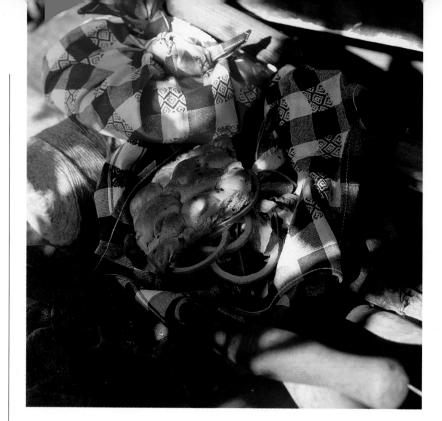

1 To make the red hot mayonnaise, first place the chillies under a preheated hot grill for 5-7 minutes, turning once, until charred and blistered. Transfer to a polythene bag, close the top lightly and set aside until cool. Rub off the charred skins, slit the chillies open and remove the seeds. Set aside.
2 Whisk the egg yolks and vinegar until slightly thickened. Continue to whisk, adding the sunflower oil in a thin steady stream until the mixture forms a thick creamy mayonnaise. Cover and set aside.
3 Place the garlic, pine nuts and Parmesan in a liquidizer or food processor and purée until smooth.

Add the sun-dried tomato halves and the red chillies and purée until smooth. With the motor running, gradually add 3 tablespoons of the reserved oil from the tomatoes. Spoon the blended mixture into a bowl, stir in the creamy mayonnaise, cover and set aside.
4 Place the turkey escalopes in a single layer in a shallow dish. Mix the olive oil and orange juice in a jug. Pour the mixture over the escalopes and turn to coat. Cover and marinate for 30-60 minutes.
5 Drain the turkey, reserving the marinade in a jug, then cook the escalopes on an oiled barbecue grill over hot coals for 3-4 minutes on

each side or until tender, basting frequently with the marinade. Remove from the heat, cut into thin strips, place in a bowl and keep hot.
6 Slice the focaccia or olive bread in half. Toast both halves, crumb side down, on the barbecue grill. Spread each half with the red mayonnaise. Divide the artichokes between the bread halves and add the red onion, rocket and sliced hot turkey. Sprinkle with salt and pepper to taste and serve at once.

Serves 4
Preparation time: 20 minutes, plus 30-60 minutes marinating time
Cooking time: 6-8 minutes

South-east Asian Grilled Chicken, with Pineapple and Peanut Relish

Like many of the best barbecue recipes, this one comes from South-east Asia.

4 part-boned chicken breasts
shredded lettuce, to serve (optional)

MARINADE:

2 sticks of lemon grass, finely chopped
juice of 2 limes
2 red chillies, deseeded and chopped
3 garlic cloves, crushed
2.5 cm/1 inch piece of fresh
    root ginger, finely chopped
2 tablespoons soft dark brown sugar
2 tablespoons chopped fresh coriander
150 ml/¼ pint coconut milk

RELISH:

1 small pineapple, peeled, cored and
    finely chopped
1 red onion, chopped
3 tablespoons freshly squeezed
    lime juice
1 garlic clove, crushed
1 tablespoon light soy sauce
25 g/1 oz roasted unsalted
    peanuts, chopped

1 Cut 3 diagonal slits in each chicken breast. Place the chicken in a shallow dish large enough to hold all the breasts in a single layer.

2 Place all the ingredients for the marinade in a liquidizer or food processor and purée until smooth. Pour over the chicken, cover and marinate for 1-1½ hours.

3 Meanwhile, to make the relish, mix all the ingredients in a bowl, cover and set aside.

4 Drain the chicken breasts, and reserve the marinade in a jug. Cook the chicken on an oiled barbecue grill over hot coals for 25-30 minutes or until cooked through.

5 Transfer to individual plates and serve with the shredded lettuce (if using) and the peanut and pineapple relish. Steamed mixed rice and a garnish of lime halves or wedges would be suitable accompaniments.

Serves 4
Preparation time: 30 minutes
Cooking time: 25-30 minutes

Rabbit with Oyster Mushrooms and Hazelnut Butter

Rabbit is delicious cooked on the barbecue — and very easy.

1 rabbit, cut into 8 portions
125 g/4 oz butter, slightly softened
50 g/2 oz hazelnuts, toasted and
  chopped
salt and pepper
SKEWERED MUSHROOMS:
250 g/8 oz oyster mushrooms,
  trimmed
8 slices of pancetta
25 g/1 oz butter, melted

MARINADE:
300 ml/½ pint dry white wine
15 g/½ oz chopped fresh tarragon
  leaves
3 tablespoons olive or hazelnut oil
strips of rind from 1 lemon
1 teaspoon black peppercorns

1 Place the rabbit portions in a single layer in a shallow dish. Mix the marinade ingredients together in a jug, pour over the rabbit and toss to coat. Cover the dish and marinate for 6-8 hours or overnight in the refrigerator.

2 Beat the butter until light and fluffy, stir in the hazelnuts, then season to taste. Lay a 25 x 25 cm/10 x 10 inch square piece of greaseproof paper on a work surface. Spoon the butter evenly down the centre, roll over the paper to form a long thin 'sausage', twist the ends and place in the refrigerator to harden.

3 Shortly before cooking the rabbit, make the skewered mushrooms. If using wooden skewers, soak them in cold water for 30 minutes. Thread the mushrooms on to 8 skewers, winding the pancetta between them. Brush with melted butter.

4 Drain the rabbit and reserve the marinade. Cook on an oiled grill over hot coals for 20-25 minutes, or until tender. Baste frequently with the marinade. Add the mushroom skewers to the grill for the final 5 minutes, turning frequently.

5 Place 2 rabbit portions on each plate, add a mushroom skewer to each and dot with slices of the hazelnut butter. Serve with grilled celery, if liked.

Serves 4
Preparation time: 10 minutes, plus 6-8 hours marinating time (or overnight)
Cooking time: 20-25 minutes

Baked Stuffed Acorn Squash

Melting buttery baby squash with couscous and fudgy grilled dates.

a generous pinch of saffron threads
400 ml/14 fl oz boiling water
250 g/8 oz quick-cooking couscous
2 large aubergines
25 g/1 oz salt
6 tablespoons olive oil
½ teaspoon ground cinnamon
125 g/4 oz pecan nuts, toasted and chopped
2 small acorn squash, cut in half lengthways, seeds removed
25 g/1 oz butter
12 medjool dates, threaded on 4 small skewers (soaked 30 minutes in water if wooden)
salt and pepper

1 Infuse the saffron for 10 minutes in the boiling water in a large heatproof bowl. Add the couscous, stir and leave to stand for 6-8 minutes, until it swells and absorbs all the water. Fluff up the grains with a fork and set aside.

2 Slice the aubergines lengthways into 1 cm/½ inch slices. Place in layers in a colander and sprinkle each layer with salt. Leave to stand for 30 minutes, rinse well under cold running water, drain and pat dry with kitchen paper.

3 Using 3 tablespoons of the olive oil, brush the aubergine on both sides. Cook under a preheated grill (or on the barbecue) for 5-6 minutes on each side, until tender. Cool slightly, cut the slices into 1 cm/½ inch strips, and add to the couscous. Add the cinnamon, pecans and seasoning. Toss well.

4 Brush the squash with the remaining oil and fill with the couscous mixture. Dot with the butter. Wrap each half in a double thickness of foil and place in the embers of the barbecue for 30 minutes or until the flesh is tender.

5 Grill the dates on a barbecue for 3-4 minutes, until golden. Turn frequently.

6 To serve, unwrap each squash and serve with a date kebab.

Serves 4
Preparation time: 1 hour
Cooking time: about 30 minutes

Hot Asparagus with Balsamic Vinegar and Tomato Dressing

Asparagus is perfect for the barbecue as it cooks quickly and easily. Serve this as a starter, with lots of warm bread to mop up the juices, while you prepare the main course. Plainly grilled, asparagus is delicious with fish, poultry or meat (see page 42).

2 tablespoons balsamic vinegar
1-2 garlic cloves, crushed
375 g/12 oz tomatoes, skinned, deseeded and chopped
7 tablespoons olive oil
500 g/1 lb young asparagus spears
50 g/2 oz pine nuts, toasted
25 g/1 oz Parmesan cheese, shaved into thin slivers
sea salt flakes and pepper

1 Place the vinegar, garlic, chopped tomatoes and 5 tablespoons of the olive oil in a small bowl. Mix well to combine and set aside.
2 Trim the asparagus spears to remove any tough fibrous stems. Brush them with the remaining olive oil and cook on an oiled barbecue grill over moderately hot coals for about 5-6 minutes, until tender.
3 Divide the grilled asparagus between 4 warmed serving plates.

Spoon over the balsamic vinegar and tomato dressing, top with the pine nuts and Parmesan slivers and sprinkle with the sea salt flakes and pepper. Serve at once.

Serves 4
Preparation time: 15 minutes
Cooking time: 5-6 minutes

Mixed Grilled Vegetables with Green Olive and Walnut Paste

Choose a selection of vegetables in season to serve with this rich green olive and walnut paste. Asparagus and fennel are also excellent when barbecued.

1 large aubergine
2 red peppers
2 yellow peppers
2 courgettes
8 baby leeks
6 tablespoons olive oil
4 large slices crusty country bread
salt and pepper
OLIVE AND WALNUT PASTE:
75 g/3 oz pitted green olives
75 g/3 oz walnut pieces
25 g/1 oz bottled pickled
   walnuts, drained
2 garlic cloves, crushed
25 g/1 oz fresh parsley
125 ml/4 fl oz extra-virgin olive oil

1 To make the olive and walnut paste, place the olives, fresh and pickled walnuts, garlic and parsley in a liquidizer or food processor and process until finely chopped. Gradually add the olive oil through the feeder tube until the mixture forms a stiff paste. Scrape into a bowl and season with salt and pepper.

2 Cut the aubergine into slices 1 cm/ ½ inch thick. Place in layers in a colander set over a plate to catch the juices. Sprinkle each layer with salt. Leave to stand for 30 minutes, then rinse under cold running water, drain well and pat dry with kitchen paper.

3 Cut the peppers in half. Remove the seeds but leave the stalk on. Slice the courgettes lengthways. Rinse the leeks well to remove any grit.

4 Brush the aubergines, courgettes and leeks with the olive oil. Place on an oiled grill over moderately hot coals. Cook the aubergine and peppers for 6-8 minutes, the courgettes and leeks for 3 minutes, turning frequently, until tender. Brush the bread with any remaining olive oil and grill until golden. Spread the toast with the olive and walnut paste and top with the vegetables.

Serves 4
Preparation time: 1 hour
Cooking time: 10 minutes

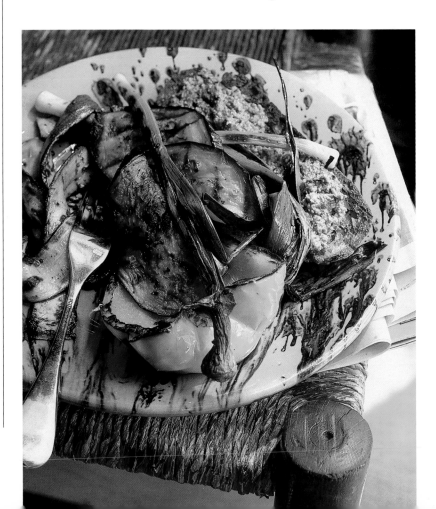

Whole Baked Sweetcorn with Skorthalia

Cobs of tender young corn, preferably freshly picked, are delicious when spread with this rich garlic sauce.

4 whole corn cobs, with husks
SKORTHALIA:
50 g/2 oz fresh white breadcrumbs
75 g/3 oz ground almonds

4 garlic cloves, crushed
2 tablespoons lemon juice
150 ml/¼ pint extra-virgin olive oil
salt and pepper

1 To make the skorthalia, place the breadcrumbs in a bowl and cover with water. Soak for 5 minutes, then squeeze out the excess liquid and place the crumbs in a liquidizer or food processor. Add the ground almonds, garlic and 1 tablespoon of the lemon juice. Process until mixed. With the motor running, gradually add the olive oil in a thin steady stream until the mixture resembles mayonnaise. Add more lemon juice and salt and pepper to taste.

2 Pull down the outer leaves of the sweetcorn husks and remove the inner silks. Pull the leaves back over the corn kernels. Place on a barbecue grill over hot coals. Cook for about 30-40 minutes until the kernels are juicy and easily come away from the core.

3 To serve, pull back the leaves of the corn cobs and spread with the skorthalia.

Serves 4
Preparation time: 15 minutes
Cooking time: 30-40 minutes

VARIATION

Grilled Baby Corn Cobs

If you are unable to obtain whole corn cobs, use baby sweetcorn instead.

1 Thread 500 g/1 lb baby corn cobs on skewers, brush them with a little olive oil and cook on an oiled barbecue grill over hot coals, turning frequently, for 4-6 minutes. Serve with the skorthalia.

Chinese Leaves Steamed with Shiitake Mushrooms

Chinese leaves are easily steamed in a parcel on the barbecue grill. Other varieties of mushrooms, such as brown chestnuts or tender oyster mushrooms, may be used instead of shiitakes.

375 g/12 oz Chinese leaves
125 g/4 oz shiitake mushrooms, finely sliced
1 cm/½ inch piece of fresh root ginger, peeled and finely shredded
1 garlic clove, crushed
½ tablespoon light soy sauce
2 teaspoons soft light brown sugar
1 green chilli, deseeded and finely chopped
1 teaspoon sesame oil
3 spring onions, finely chopped

1 Shred the leaves into 1 cm/½ inch strips and place in a large bowl.

2 Mix all the other ingredients in a separate bowl. Add to the Chinese leaves and toss lightly.

3 Place a large piece of doubled foil on a work surface, then pile the mixture in the centre. Bring up the edges and press to seal. Cook the foil parcel on a barbecue grill over hot coals for 5-10 minutes, shaking occasionally, until the Chinese leaves and mushrooms are tender.

Serves 4
Preparation time: 10 minutes
Cooking time: 5-10 minutes

Red Bean and Rice Patties

125 g/4 oz red kidney beans
125 g/4 oz brown rice
1 tablespoon groundnut oil
1 onion, finely chopped
1 garlic clove, crushed
1 green chilli, deseeded and
    finely chopped
1 teaspoon cumin seeds
1 teaspoon ground coriander
½ teaspoon ground turmeric
2 eggs, beaten
salt and pepper
SAUCE:
3 tablespoons chopped fresh
    coriander
25 g/1 oz pistachio nuts, chopped
2 green chillies, deseeded and
    finely chopped
125 ml/4 fl oz Greek yogurt

1 Place the beans in a bowl, cover with cold water and leave to soak overnight. Drain, rinse in a colander under cold running water and drain. Place the beans in a saucepan, cover with fresh water and boil vigorously for 10 minutes. Lower the heat and simmer for 50-60 minutes, until tender. Drain, set aside to cool, then mash until smooth.

2 Bring a small saucepan of lightly salted water to the boil, add the rice, lower the heat and simmer for about 20-25 minutes until the grains are just cooked. Drain, refresh under cold running water, then drain well.

3 Heat the oil in a small frying pan, add the onion, garlic and chilli and cook for 5 minutes without browning the onion. Add the cumin seeds, coriander and turmeric and cook for about 1-2 minutes more, then add the contents of the frying pan to the mashed beans. Stir in the rice and mix together well. Add the eggs, and salt and pepper to taste, then mix well to combine.

4 To make the sauce, place the coriander, the pistachios and the green chillies in a liquidizer or food processor and purée until smooth. Scrape the mixture into a bowl, stir in the yogurt and season to taste.

5 Divide the bean and rice mixture into 4 equal portions and shape into flat rounds. Brush each round with a little oil, then place on a well-oiled barbecue grill and cook over moderately hot coals for about 4-5 minutes, until a crisp crust has formed, then turn them over and cook for a further 4-5 minutes.

6 Serve the patties with the sauce, a crisp leafy salad and fresh limes, cut into wedges.

Serves 4
Preparation time: 1 hour 30 minutes, plus overnight soaking
Cooking time: 10 minutes

Polenta and Vegetable Terrine with Roasted Tomatoes

4 tablespoons olive oil, plus extra
  for brushing
1 red pepper
250 g/8 oz mushrooms, quartered
2 red onions, cut into small wedges
125 g/4 oz baby courgettes, cut in
  half lengthways
125 g/4 oz baby carrots
125 g/4 oz French beans, topped
  and tailed

125 g/4 oz broccoli, cut into florets
1.5 litres/2½ pints water
300 g/10 oz polenta
50 g/2 oz Parmesan cheese, grated,
  plus extra for sprinkling
2 garlic cloves, crushed
8 ripe plum tomatoes, cut in
  half lengthways
50 g/2 oz black olives
salt and pepper

1 Brush a 1.25 kg/2½ lb loaf tin with olive oil. Place the red pepper under a preheated grill for 10 minutes until blistered and charred. Place in a polythene bag, close lightly and set aside to cool. Peel off the charred skin, cut the pepper in half and remove the seeds. Cut the flesh into 2.5 cm/1 inch wide strips.
2 Heat half the oil in a frying pan, add the mushrooms and onions, cover and cook for 2-3 minutes. Remove with a slotted spoon and drain on kitchen paper.
3 Blanch the remaining vegetables in separate saucepans of boiling salted water until crisp and tender. Drain, refresh under cold running water and drain well.
4 Bring the measured water to the boil in a large saucepan. Add a pinch of salt, then pour in the polenta in a thin steady stream, stirring all the time. Continue to stir the mixture (beating it as it thickens) for about 20 minutes until it leaves the sides of the pan. Remove from the heat, add all the vegetables and the grated Parmesan, mix well and spoon into the loaf tin. Level the surface and set aside. When the polenta loaf is completely cold, turn it out of the tin and cut it into 2 cm/¾ inch slices. Brush each side with a little of the remaining oil.
5 Mix the remaining oil and garlic, brush over the tomatoes and season to taste.
6 Place the terrine slices on an oiled barbecue grill over moderately hot coals. Add the tomatoes, cut side down. Cook the terrine and tomatoes for 6-8 minutes, turning once. (Be sure the slices have a crispy surface before turning.)
7 Serve the terrine on individual plates topped with the tomato halves. Garnish with the olives and serve with more grated Parmesan.

Serves 6-8
Preparation time: 1 hour 10 minutes
Cooking time: 6-8 minutes

VARIATION
Polenta and Vegetable Kebabs

1 Make the polenta as in the main recipe. As soon as it leaves the sides of the pan, pour out into a mound on a board. Leave to cool, then cut into 2.5 cm/1 inch cubes.
2 Thread the cubes of polenta on to skewers, alternating with the raw red onions, mushrooms, squares of red pepper, thickly sliced courgettes and blanched carrots. Brush with olive oil. Grill for about 5-6 minutes on each side over moderately hot coals until the vegetables are tender and the polenta cubes are golden.
3 Serve with the grilled tomato halves and sprinkle with Parmesan.

Baby Aubergines with Herbed Greek Yogurt

Mini vegetables are perfect for cooking whole on the barbecue as they are usually sweet and tender, so cook speedily. Little aubergines are usually available in ethnic markets. Make the yogurt mixture well ahead, so the flavours mix thoroughly, then serve these baby aubergines with warm pitta bread lightly toasted on the grill.

12 baby aubergines
3 tablespoons olive oil
salt and pepper

HERBED GREEK YOGURT:
2 tablespoons chopped fresh parsley
2 tablespoons chopped fresh dill
2 tablespoons chopped fresh mint
1 small red onion, finely chopped
2 garlic cloves, crushed
75 g/3 oz Kalamata olives, pitted and sliced
2 teaspoons fennel seeds, crushed
1 tablespoon capers, chopped
15 g/½ oz gherkins, finely chopped
finely grated rind and juice of 1 lime
150 ml/¼ pint strained Greek yogurt
salt and pepper

1 To make the herbed Greek yogurt, mix all the ingredients and set aside.
2 Slice all the baby aubergines in half lengthways, leaving the aubergines attached to their stalks.
3 Using a small brush, coat the aubergines with olive oil. Cook on an oiled barbecue grill over moderately hot coals for about 2-3 minutes on each side.
4 To serve, place the aubergines on a serving dish or plate and spoon over the herbed yogurt.

Serves 4
Preparation time: 20 minutes
Cooking time: 6 minutes

Baby Brioche Florentine with Hollandaise Sauce

Serve these stuffed brioche at a breakfast or brunch barbecue with crispy grilled bacon.

25 g/1 oz butter
250 g/1 lb young leaf spinach
grated nutmeg, to taste
8 baby brioche rolls
8 quails' eggs

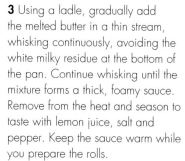

HOLLANDAISE SAUCE:
175 g/6 oz butter
3 egg yolks
2 tablespoons water
1 tablespoon lemon juice or to taste
salt and pepper

1 To make the hollandaise sauce, first melt the butter in a small pan over a low heat. Cool slightly.
2 Mix the egg yolks and water in a large heatproof bowl. Set this over a large saucepan of barely simmering water. Whisk until light, creamy and pale in colour.

3 Using a ladle, gradually add the melted butter in a thin stream, whisking continuously, avoiding the white milky residue at the bottom of the pan. Continue whisking until the mixture forms a thick, foamy sauce. Remove from the heat and season to taste with lemon juice, salt and pepper. Keep the sauce warm while you prepare the rolls.
4 Melt the butter in a large saucepan. Wash the spinach and add it to the pan with only the water that clings to the leaves. Cover the pan and cook for about 3-4 minutes, stirring once, until the spinach has just wilted. Drain well and transfer to a bowl. Add salt and plenty of nutmeg and pepper, to taste.
5 Cut a neat slice off the top of each brioche roll. Set the 'lids' aside, then remove sufficient crumb from the centre of each roll to create a hollow. Place a spoonful of spinach in each hollow and carefully crack a quail's egg over the top. Replace the brioche lids. Wrap each roll in a double thickness of foil and place right side up on a barbecue grill. Cook for 30-40 minutes, until the eggs are just set.
6 Serve immediately on individual plates, with the hollandaise sauce.

Serves 4
Preparation time: 15 minutes
Cooking time: 30-40 minutes

Goats' Cheese in Vine Leaves

Goats' cheese is delicious when wrapped and grilled in vine leaves. Choose small whole cheeses such as crottin and serve the oozing cheese on toast with a salad or selection of grilled vegetables.

4-8 vine leaves, fresh or preserved in brine	1 tablespoon chopped fresh oregano
1 tablespoon chopped fresh thyme leaves	1 teaspoon crushed mixed peppercorns
1 tablespoon chopped fresh flat leaf parsley	1 tablespoon lemon juice
	4 small whole goats' cheeses
	2 tablespoons olive oil

1 If using vine leaves preserved in brine, rinse them well in a colander under cold running water. Bring a small saucepan of water to the boil, add the vine leaves and blanch for 1 minute. If using fresh vine leaves, remove any tough stems and blanch briefly in boiling water for 30 seconds. Regardless of type, refresh the blanched leaves under cold water, then drain well.

2 Mix the chopped fresh herbs with the crushed peppercorns and lemon juice in a shallow bowl. Brush the goats' cheeses with olive oil and roll them in the herb mixture. Wrap the coated cheeses in the vine leaves, then brush them with any remaining olive oil.

3 Place the wrapped goats' cheeses on an oiled barbecue grill over moderately hot coals. Cook for 8 minutes, turning once, until the cheeses are just soft. Serve with toasted crusty bread, salad or grilled vegetables, such as peppers.

Serves 4
Preparation time: 10 minutes
Cooking time: 8 minutes

VARIATION

Haloumi Parcels

1 Greek haloumi cheese may be used instead of goats' cheese, if preferred. Cut the cheese into quarters and brush with olive oil. Mix the chopped herbs, crushed peppercorns and lemon juice, roll the cheese quarters in the mixture, wrap them in vine leaves and proceed as in the main recipe.

Baked Beetroot with Mustard and Walnut Sauce

Beetroot is a delicious hot vegetable, especially served with this creamy mustard sauce.

8 raw beetroot

MUSTARD AND WALNUT SAUCE:

75 g/3 oz walnut halves
175 g/6 oz crème fraîche
1½ tablespoons wholegrain mustard
3 tablespoons snipped chives, plus extra for garnish
salt and pepper

1 Roast the walnuts on a baking sheet in a preheated oven at 180°C (350°F), Gas Mark 4, for about 8-10 minutes, until golden. Leave to cool, then chop roughly. Reserve 3 tablespoons of the nuts for garnish, and put the rest in a bowl.
2 Stir in the crème fraîche, mustard and snipped chives. Season with salt and pepper to taste.
3 Wrap each beetroot in a double thickness of foil. Place in the embers of the hot barbecue and cook for about 40-50 minutes, or until tender.
4 Unwrap the foil, split open the beetroot and top with the sauce, the reserved walnuts and extra chives.

Serves 4
Preparation time: 15 minutes
Cooking time: 40-50 minutes

Grilled Radicchio with Pears and Roquefort

The slight bitterness of the radicchio combines well with citrus-sweet baked pears and creamy sharp cheese to make a dish which is equally suitable as an unusual starter or as an ending to a rich meal. Sadly the ruby red colour of the radicchio is somewhat lost in cooking but the flavour is delicious none the less.

4 ripe pears, such as Conference
finely grated rind and juice of
  2 oranges
4 tablespoons clear honey
4 small radicchio
1 tablespoon walnut oil
125 g/4 oz Roquefort cheese,
  crumbled
pepper

1 Cut each pear into quarters lengthways and remove the cores. Place the pears in a single layer on a large sheet of double foil, turning up the edges slightly.

2 Mix the orange rind and juice and honey in a jug. Pour over the pears.

3 Bring up the edges of the foil and press together to seal. Place the parcel on a barbecue grill over moderately hot coals and cook for about 15-20 minutes or until the pears are tender.

4 About 6 minutes before the pears are ready, cook the radicchio. Cut each radicchio into quarters, brush with the walnut oil and cook on the grill for 2-3 minutes on each side.

5 To serve, divide the pears and their cooking juices between 4 plates. Add 4 radicchio quarters to each portion then sprinkle the radicchio with the crumbled Roquefort and a little pepper.

Serves 4
Preparation time: 5 minutes
Cooking time: 15-20 minutes

VARIATION

Pears and Roquefort with Almonds

1 Prepare the pears as for the main recipe. Before closing the foil parcel, sprinkle 125 g/4 oz crumbled Roquefort cheese over the pears. When ready to serve, strew each portion with toasted almonds.

Black Bean Kebabs with Mango Relish

125 g/4 oz dried black beans
3 tablespoons olive oil
1 onion, very finely chopped
1 garlic clove, crushed
1 red chilli, deseeded and
    finely chopped
½ teaspoon ground cumin
½ teaspoon ground coriander
1 tablespoon chopped fresh coriander
2 medium courgettes

24 mixed red and yellow
    cherry tomatoes
MANGO RELISH:
1 ripe mango
1 small onion, grated
1 red chilli, deseeded and
    finely chopped
1 cm/½ inch piece of fresh root
    ginger, peeled and grated
salt and pepper

1 Place the beans in a bowl with cold water to cover. Soak overnight, then tip into a colander and rinse well under cold running water. Transfer to a saucepan and cover with fresh water. Bring to the boil. Boil vigorously for 10 minutes, then lower the heat and simmer for about 40-50 minutes, or until tender. Drain well and set the beans aside.

2 To make the mango relish, first peel the mango and cut the flesh away from the stone. Place the flesh in a bowl and mash lightly with a fork. Add the onion, chilli and ginger and mix well. Season with a little salt and pepper and set aside.

3 Heat 2 tablespoons of the oil in a frying pan. Add the onion, garlic and chilli and cook gently for 5-10 minutes, until the onion is softened but not coloured. Stir in the cumin and ground coriander and cook for 1-2 minutes more.

4 Turn the onion and spice mixture into a bowl, add the drained beans and fresh coriander and mash well. Divide the mixture into 24 and roll into balls.

5 Using a potato peeler, cut the courgette lengthways into strips. Brush with the remaining oil. Thread the bean balls on metal skewers, alternating with the cherry tomatoes and weaving the courgette strips in between.

6 Cook the kebabs on a well-oiled barbecue grill over moderately hot coals for 4 minutes on each side. Serve with the mango relish and rice.

Serves 4
Preparation time: 1 hour 20 minutes, plus overnight soaking
Cooking time: 8 minutes

VARIATION

Apricot Relish

This apricot relish, or the papaya relish on page 60, are also delicious with the black bean kebabs.

8 ripe apricots
2 tablespoons chopped red onion
1-2 green chillies, deseeded
    and chopped
½ tablespoon walnut oil
salt and pepper

1 Score a cross on the top of each apricot. Plunge them into a saucepan of boiling water for 20 seconds, then, using a slotted spoon, transfer them to a bowl of cold water. Slip off the skins, cut the apricots in half and discard the stones. Chop the flesh finely and place it in a bowl with the onion, chillies and walnut oil. Mix well and season to taste.

Stuffed Mini Peppers with Tomato Sauce

Miniature peppers, stuffed with a creamy minted cheese, are delicious with plain grilled chicken or as a starter.

8 mini peppers
Greek yogurt, to serve
STUFFING:
125 g/4 oz soft fresh goats' cheese
50 g/2 oz ricotta
1½ tablespoons chopped fresh mint
1 red or green chilli, deseeded and
    finely chopped (optional)
salt and pepper
TOMATO SAUCE:
1 tablespoon olive oil
1 onion, finely chopped
1 garlic clove, crushed
1 x 425 g/14 oz can tomatoes
1 tablespoon chopped fresh parsley
1 tablespoon chopped fresh oregano

1 To make the sauce, heat the oil in a saucepan, add the onion and the garlic and cook for 5 minutes, until softened but not coloured. Stir in the canned tomatoes and herbs and simmer gently for 10 minutes. Strain the sauce through a sieve set over a clean pan. Set aside.

2 To make the stuffing, combine the goats' cheese, ricotta and mint in a bowl. Stir in the chilli, if using, and season to taste.

3 Make a small slit in the side of each pepper, carefully scrape out the seeds and core with a teaspoon, keeping the pepper shells intact. Half fill each pepper with stuffing – do not be tempted to fill them completely, or they may burst during cooking.

4 Cook the filled peppers on an oiled barbecue grill over moderately hot coals for about 10-15 minutes, turning occasionally, until softened.

Meanwhile, reheat the tomato sauce by placing the pan at the edge of the barbecue grill.

5 Place 2 of the filled peppers on each plate and serve with the tomato sauce and a generous spoonful of Greek yogurt, if liked.

Serves 4
Preparation time: 20 minutes
Cooking time: 10-15 minutes

Grilled Sweet Potato and Aïoli

Aïoli, or garlic mayonnaise, is served here with delicious nutty sweet potatoes. You could also add 15 g/½ oz chopped fresh mixed herbs to the aïoli.

500 g/1 lb sweet potatoes, scrubbed
4 tablespoons olive oil
salt and pepper
AIOLI:
4-6 garlic cloves, crushed
2 egg yolks
juice of ½ lemon, plus extra, to taste
300 ml/½ pint extra-virgin olive oil

1 To make the aïoli, place the garlic and egg yolks in a liquidizer or food processor, add the lemon juice and process briefly to mix. With the motor running, gradually add the olive oil in a thin steady stream until the mixture forms a thick cream. Add salt and pepper to taste and stir in more lemon juice if liked. Scrape the aïoli into a bowl and set aside.
2 To prepare the sweet potatoes, cut each potato into 5 mm/¼ inch slices, brush with the olive oil and place on an oiled barbecue grill over moderately hot coals. Grill for about 5 minutes on each side until tender. Serve hot with the aïoli.

Serves 4
Preparation time: 15 minutes
Cooking time: 10 minutes

Raw Beetroot and Pink Grapefruit Salad

A scrumptious union of crunchy raw beetroot, sweet pink grapefruit and hazelnuts makes a pretty and stunning salad!

750 g/1½ lb raw young beetroot
2 pink grapefruit
50 g/2 oz peeled hazelnuts, roasted and coarsely chopped
1 tablespoon raspberry vinegar
3 tablespoons hazelnut oil
1 garlic clove, crushed
1 radicchio, leaves separated
250 g/8 oz young spinach leaves
salt and pepper

1 Peel the beetroot, then cut it into fine julienne strips or grate it finely. Place in a salad bowl.

2 Cut a thin slice off the bottom of the grapefruit and place them, cut side down, on a board. Cut off the rind in strips, working from the top down. Take care to remove all the white pith. Holding the grapefruit over the salad bowl to catch any juice, cut out the segments with a knife. Add the segments to the bowl, stir in the hazelnuts and toss lightly.

3 Whisk the raspberry vinegar, hazelnut oil and garlic in a small bowl; pour over the beetroot mixture, add salt and pepper to taste and toss well. Arrange the radicchio and spinach leaves on individual plates and spoon over the beetroot, hazelnut and grapefruit mixture.

Serves 4-6
Preparation time: 20 minutes

Kohlrabi and Bean Sprout Salad

A fresh, crisp salad of crunchy bean sprouts and kohlrabi – a vegetable with a sweet, nutty flavour, similar to turnip.

75 g/3 oz unsalted cashew nuts
75 g/3 oz grated fresh coconut
   or 50 g/2 oz unsweetened
   desiccated coconut
250 g/8 oz kohlrabi
125 g/4 oz fresh bean sprouts,
   rinsed and dried
3 spring onions, finely chopped
1 tablespoon chopped fresh mint
1 garlic clove, crushed
2 tablespoons freshly squeezed
   lime juice
2 tablespoons clear honey

1 Spread out the cashew nuts on a baking sheet. Place in a preheated oven, 180°C (350°F), Gas Mark 4, for 10-15 minutes, until the nuts are evenly golden. Leave to cool, then chop coarsely.

2 If using desiccated coconut, place in a bowl with warm water to cover. Leave to soak for 20 minutes, then strain through a sieve, pressing the coconut against the sides with the back of a spoon to squeeze out any excess moisture.

3 Peel the kohlrabi and grate it coarsely into a bowl. Add the bean sprouts, coconut, spring onions and mint. Mix well.

4 Combine the garlic, lime juice and honey in a jug. Mix thoroughly, then pour over the salad. Toss lightly, sprinkle with the chopped cashew nuts and serve.

Serves 4-6
Preparation time: 20 minutes

Celery and Fennel Salad with Blue Cheese Dressing

Fennel, with its light aniseed flavour, is delicious combined with celery, pears and pecan nuts in this salad.

75 g/3 oz Roquefort or
    Gorgonzola cheese
50 g/2 oz crème fraîche or
    soured cream
1 tablespoon red wine vinegar
3 spring onions, finely sliced
75 g/3 oz pecan nuts, finely chopped
2 pears
½ tablespoon lemon juice
1 fennel bulb, trimmed and finely sliced
4 celery sticks, finely sliced
pepper
escarole lettuce and watercress,
    to serve

1 Place the blue cheese, crème fraîche or soured cream and vinegar in a liquidizer or food processor and purée until smooth. Alternatively, mix in a bowl and mash with a fork. Stir in the spring onions, 50 g/2 oz of the pecans and pepper to taste.
2 Cut the pears in half and remove the cores. Cut the flesh into cubes, place in a bowl and mix with the lemon juice. Add the sliced fennel and celery to the pears.
3 To serve, arrange the salad leaves on individual serving plates or bowls.

Top with the fennel, celery and pear mixture, spoon over the blue cheese dressing and sprinkle with the remaining pecans.

Serves 4-6
Preparation time: 20 minutes

Orecchiette, Broad Bean and Pecorino Salad

'Orecchiette', meaning 'little ears', are pasta shapes with a soft creamy texture and go very well with this mixture of sharp Pecorino cheese and sweet baby broad beans.

750 g/1½ lb fresh young broad beans
    in the pod or 250 g/8 oz frozen
    broad beans, thawed
5 tablespoons extra-virgin olive oil
500 g/1 lb orecchiette or similar short
    pasta shapes
75 g/3 oz Pecorino cheese, grated

50 g/2 oz pitted black olives,
    finely chopped
5 tablespoons chopped fresh
    flat leaf parsley
1 tablespoon balsamic vinegar
salt and pepper

1 Shell the broad beans, if fresh. Bring a saucepan of lightly salted water to the boil, add the fresh or thawed frozen beans and blanch for 1 minute. Drain, refresh under cold water, then drain again. Pop the beans out of their skins.
2 Bring a large saucepan of boiling water to the boil with a little oil and salt, drop in the pasta and cook for 12-15 minutes, or until just tender. Drain the pasta in a colander, refresh under cold water and drain thoroughly.
3 Tip the pasta into a large salad bowl and add the remaining ingredients. Toss well, add plenty of pepper and serve.

Serves 4
Preparation time: 20 minutes

Yellow Pepper and Chicory Salad with Caesar Dressing

Anchovies make a marvellous addition to all kinds of salads and here they are the perfect complement to the smoky flavour of grilled peppers in this special-occasion dish.

4 yellow peppers
oil for shallow frying
3-4 slices of white bread, torn into
    1 cm/½ inch pieces
1 cos lettuce, leaves separated, torn
    into pieces if large
2 heads of chicory, leaves separated
DRESSING:
2 garlic cloves, crushed
1 egg yolk
1-2 tablespoons lemon juice
1 teaspoon Worcestershire sauce
8-10 canned anchovy fillets,
    drained and mashed
4 tablespoons olive oil
25 g/1 oz Parmesan cheese, finely
    grated, plus extra for sprinkling
crushed black peppercorns

1 Place the yellow peppers under a preheated hot grill. Cook for about 10-15 minutes, turning occasionally, until blistered and charred. Transfer the peppers to a polythene bag, close the top lightly and set aside until the peppers are cool. Peel off the charred skin, then cut the peppers in half and remove the seeds. Cut the flesh into long strips and set aside on a plate.

2 To make the dressing, combine the garlic, egg yolk, 1 tablespoon of the lemon juice, Worcestershire sauce and anchovies in a bowl and whisk until slightly thickened. Add the olive oil in a thin stream, whisking continuously until the mixture forms a thick cream. Stir in the Parmesan and season with pepper. Taste and add more lemon juice if liked.

3 Heat the oil for shallow frying in a frying pan. Add the bread pieces and cook until evenly golden, then remove with a slotted spoon and drain on kitchen paper.

4 Place the lettuce and chicory leaves in a bowl with the strips of yellow pepper. Pour over the dressing and toss lightly. To serve, sprinkle with the croûtons and a little extra Parmesan cheese.

Serves 4
Preparation time: 30 minutes
Cooking time: 10-15 minutes

Cucumber, Radish and Dill Salad

2 cucumbers
6 tablespoons sea salt
1 bunch of radishes, trimmed and
    thinly sliced
1 egg yolk
1 tablespoon coarsegrain mustard
1 tablespoon clear honey
2 tablespoons lemon juice
3 tablespoons olive oil
3 tablespoons chopped fresh dill
pepper

1 Cut both the cucumbers in half lengthways, scoop out the seeds if bitter and slice very thinly.
2 Layer the cucumber slices in a colander and sprinkle with the salt. Set the colander over a plate or in the sink to catch the juices and leave for 1-1½ hours. Rinse well under cold water, drain and pat the slices dry with a clean tea towel. Place in a salad bowl and add the radishes.
3 Place the egg yolk in a small bowl with the mustard, honey, pepper and lemon juice. Whisk well to combine. Continue to whisk while gradually adding the oil in a thin stream until well amalgamated. Stir in the chopped dill. Add to the cucumber and radishes, toss well and serve.

Serves 4-6
Preparation time: 15 minutes, plus
1-1½ hours for salting cucumbers
and 1-1½ hours marinating time

Tabbouleh and Fennel Salad

Fennel adds crunch to this light moist salad made with bulgar wheat.

250 g/8 oz bulgar wheat
1 bulb of fennel, very finely sliced
1 red onion, finely sliced
5 tablespoons chopped fresh mint
5 tablespoons chopped fresh parsley

2 teaspoons fennel seeds, crushed
2 tablespoons olive oil
finely grated rind and juice
   of 2 lemons
salt and pepper

1 Place the bulgar wheat in a bowl, add enough cold water to cover, then leave to stand for 30 minutes, until all the water has been absorbed. Line a colander with muslin or a clean tea towel. Drain the bulgar wheat into the colander, then gather up the sides of the cloth or towel and squeeze to extract as much of the liquid as possible from the bulgar wheat. Tip the wheat into a salad bowl.
2 Stir in the fennel, onion, mint, parsley, fennel seeds, oil, lemon rind and half the lemon juice. Add salt and pepper to taste. Cover and set aside for 30 minutes, then taste the salad and add more lemon juice if required.

Serves 6
Preparation time: 35 minutes, plus 30 minutes soaking time

VARIATION

Couscous and Celery Salad

1 Substitute 250 g/8 oz quick-cooking couscous for the bulgar wheat and 6 celery sticks, finely sliced, for the fennel. Proceed as in the main recipe.

Carrot and Celeriac Salad

Crisp carrots and nutty celeriac blend well with a mild, peppery, mustard dressing.

250 g/8 oz carrots
250 g/8 oz celeriac
6 spring onions, finely sliced
2 tablespoons sesame oil
2 teaspoons yellow mustard seeds
1 tablespoon light soy sauce
2 tablespoons freshly squeezed
    lime juice
pepper

1 Cut the carrot and celeriac into thin julienne strips or grate them coarsely. Place in a bowl with the spring onions.
2 Heat the oil gently in a small frying pan. Add the mustard seeds. When they start to pop, remove the pan from the heat – be careful not to burn them or they will become bitter. Add the mustard seeds to the carrot and celeriac mixture.
3 Mix the soy sauce and lime juice in a small bowl, add plenty of pepper and pour over the salad. Toss well and serve.

Serves 4-6
Preparation time: 10-15 minutes

Watercress and Pomegranate Salad

This is a colourful and unusual salad, perfumed with fragrant rosewater and strewn with pomegranate seeds and orange segments. It is a stunning accompaniment to barbecued meat and game. Some people are allergic to pink peppercorns, so you may wish to substitute green ones instead.

1 pomegranate
1 bunch of watercress, broken into sprigs
4 oranges
1 teaspoon rosewater
5 tablespoons olive oil
1 tablespoon raspberry vinegar
½ teaspoon drained bottled pink peppercorns in brine (see introduction, left)
sea salt flakes

1 Break open the pomegranate and remove the seeds, discarding the bitter yellow pith. Place the seeds in a large bowl with the watercress.

2 Finely grate the rind from 2 of the oranges and set aside. Segment all the oranges, as described in the recipe for Sole with Fruit, Flambéed with Pernod on page 12, catching any juices in the bowl containing the pomegranate and watercress.

3 In a separate bowl, combine the rosewater, olive oil, raspberry vinegar, pink peppercorns and reserved grated orange rind. Mix well, pour over the salad and season with a few sea salt flakes and serve.

Serves 4
Preparation time: 15 minutes

Baby Corn, Spring Onion and Coriander Salad

Crunchy little corn cobs in a dressing of spring onion, coriander and soy sauce make a memorable salad.

500 g/1 lb baby corn cobs, trimmed
2 tablespoons sesame seeds
6 spring onions, finely sliced
50 g/2 oz fresh coriander, chopped
50 ml/2 fl oz sunflower oil
2 teaspoons sesame oil

2 tablespoons freshly squeezed lime or lemon juice
1 tablespoon soy sauce
1-2 red chillies, deseeded and finely chopped (optional)
salt and pepper

1 Bring a large saucepan of lightly salted water to the boil, add the corn and cook for 3-4 minutes, until just tender. Drain in a colander, refresh under cold water and drain again well.
2 Place the sesame seeds in a dry frying pan. Heat, tossing, for 1-2 minutes, until evenly browned. Remove from the heat and set aside.
3 Mix the rest of the ingredients in a salad bowl, add the corn and toss lightly. Sprinkle with the toasted sesame seeds and serve with crusty bread.

Serves 4-6
Preparation time: 20 minutes
Cooking time: 3-4 minutes

Warm Sweet Potato and Walnut Salad

Sweet potatoes and walnuts have an affinity for each other, as is demonstrated in this simple salad.

500 g/1 lb sweet potatoes
5 tablespoons walnut oil
1 tablespoon white wine vinegar
1 shallot, finely chopped
1 garlic clove, crushed
50 g/2 oz walnuts, chopped
50 g/2 oz seedless raisins
salt and pepper

1 Peel the sweet potatoes, cut them in half lengthways, then cut across into 1 cm/½ inch slices.
2 Bring a saucepan of lightly salted water to the boil, add the sweet potatoes and cook for 5 minutes, until just tender. Drain well.
3 Mix the walnut oil, vinegar, shallot and garlic together in a large bowl. Add the warm sweet potatoes, walnuts and raisins and toss well. Add salt and pepper to taste and serve warm or chilled.

Serves 4
Preparation time: 15 minutes
Cooking time: 5 minutes

Black and White Chilli Bean Salad

Ingredients from South American cuisine are the inspiration for this colourful salad. Nutritious beans, hot chillies, aromatic coriander, lime and tomato produce a colourful dish.

125 g/4 oz dried black kidney beans
125 g/4 oz dried haricot beans
1 red onion, finely chopped
4 tomatoes, skinned and chopped
2 red chillies, deseeded and
  finely chopped
1 bunch of coriander, finely chopped
2 garlic cloves, crushed
50 ml/2 fl oz olive oil
finely grated rind and juice of 2 limes
salt and pepper

1 Place the kidney beans and the haricot beans in separate bowls and cover with cold water – use large bowls, because the beans will swell a good deal. Set aside and leave to soak overnight.

2 The next day, drain the beans and rinse them well, then place the two varieties in separate saucepans. Add cold water to cover and bring to the boil. Boil vigorously for 10 minutes, then reduce the heat and simmer the kidney beans for 50-60 minutes and the haricot beans for 45-50 minutes. When just tender, drain both beans, then refresh them under cold running water and drain again well. Place the beans in a salad bowl and mix well together.

3 Add the onion, tomatoes, chillies, coriander and garlic to the bean mixture and stir carefully to combine.

4 To make the dressing, pour the olive oil and lime rind and juice into a small bowl or jug and mix well.

5 To serve, pour the dressing over the bean salad, then taste and adjust the seasoning, adding salt and plenty of pepper. Toss well, and serve warm or cold.

Serves 6
Preparation time: 15 minutes, plus overnight soaking
Cooking time: 45 minutes-1¼ hours

Figs and Blackberries on Toast

Hot squidgy figs and blackberries baked in liqueur are served with crispy cinnamon brioche toast to mop up the delicious cooking juices. Great for dessert or a barbecue brunch.

12 ripe figs
125 g/4 oz blackberries
pared rind and juice of 2 oranges
2 tablespoons crème de cassis
1 tablespoon caster sugar
½ teaspoon cinnamon
25 g/1 oz butter, melted
4 slices brioche or white bread
fromage frais or Greek yogurt, to serve (optional)

1 Cut the figs into quarters, slicing almost but not all the way through, so the quarters fall back like flower petals. Cut 4 squares of double-thickness foil and place 3 figs and a quarter of the blackberries on each.

2 Cut the orange rind into thin julienne strips. Place in a bowl, stir in the orange juice and crème de cassis and divide between the fig parcels. Bring up the edges of the foil and press to seal.

3 Mix the sugar, cinnamon and melted butter in a bowl and brush over one side of each brioche or bread slice.

4 Cook the fig parcels on a barbecue grill over moderately hot coals for about 8-10 minutes, or until the figs are hot and slightly soft. Towards the end of the cooking time, add the buttered brioche or bread slices to the grill, with the buttered side up, and toast until golden.

5 Serve the cinnamon toast on individual plates, topped with the figs and blackberries. Add a spoonful of fromage frais or Greek yogurt, if liked.

Serves 4
Preparation time: 5-10 minutes
Cooking time: 8-10 minutes

Melon and Rosewater Granita

A fresh icy granita is perfect as a light dessert after a rich main dish, or served between courses to clear the palate. Although time consuming, it is extremely easy to make.

2 Charentais or rock melons
75 g/3 oz caster sugar
175 ml/6 fl oz water
½ teaspoon rosewater
fromage frais, to serve (optional)

1 Cut the melons in half, remove the seeds and scoop out the flesh into a liquidizer or food processor.
2 Place the sugar and measured water in a saucepan and heat for about 1-2 minutes until the sugar has dissolved. Increase the heat and boil for another 2 minutes without stirring, then remove from the heat and leave to cool slightly.
3 Add half the sugar syrup to the melon flesh and blend until smooth. Pour into a bowl and stir in the rosewater and more sugar syrup to taste; the amount needed will depend on the sweetness of the fruit.
4 Pour the melon mixture into a 25 x 15 cm/10 x 6 inch tin and place it in the refrigerator to chill. When the melon mixture is quite cold, transfer the tin to the freezer for about 1 hour or until ice crystals have formed around the rim and the mixture is starting to freeze on the base. Scrape the mixture with a fork, combining well with any liquid, then replace in the freezer. Repeat every 45 minutes until uniform crystals have formed, about 4-5 hours. Serve at once or within 4-6 hours. Spoon into glasses and top with a dollop of fromage frais, if liked.

Serves 4-6
Preparation time:10 minutes, plus 4-5 hours freezing time
Cooking time: approximately 5 minutes

Exotic Ruby Fruit Salad with Cardamom

This beautiful, crimson fruit salad is flavoured with cardamom, a fragrant spice often used in Indian, Middle Eastern and North African cooking. The flavour will be enhanced and the fruit will take on an even deeper red if the salad is left to macerate for 2-3 hours before serving.

1.5 kg/3 lb tropical fruits
    (e.g. mango, papaya, pineapple,
    lychee, tamarillo, guava or physalis)
    or other fruits of your choice
4 green cardamom pods
300 ml/½ pint freshly squeezed,
    ruby red orange juice
1 tablespoon Grand Marnier
    or Cointreau

1 Prepare all the fruit according to type. Cut into bite-sized pieces and place in a serving bowl.
2 Split open the cardamom pods, take out the little black seeds and grind them finely with a mortar and pestle. Sprinkle over the fruit.
3 Combine the orange juice and liqueur in a jug, pour over the fruit and stir well to coat.

Serves 4-6
Preparation time: 15 minutes

Baked Bananas with Cinnamon and Rum Mascarpone Cream

I first tasted baked bananas in Thailand where they were sold freshly grilled at small roadside stalls. Hot and deliciously sweet, with just a squeeze of fresh lime juice, they must be just about the best fast food ever invented! In this version they are served with a cinnamon and rum mascarpone cream.

1-2 tablespoons caster sugar
½ teaspoon ground cinnamon
2 teaspoons rum

250 g/8 oz mascarpone
8 small bananas

1 Mix the sugar, cinnamon and rum in a bowl. Stir in the mascarpone, mix well and set aside.
2 Place the whole unpeeled bananas on a barbecue grill over hot coals. Cook for 10-12 minutes, turning the bananas as the skins darken, until they are black all over and the flesh is very tender.
3 To serve, split the bananas open and spread the flesh with the cinnamon and rum mascarpone cream.

Serves 4
Preparation time: 5 minutes
Cooking time: 10-12 minutes

VARIATION

Baked Bananas with Chocolate Ricotta Cream

250 g/8 oz ricotta
1-2 tablespoons maple syrup
25 g/1 oz chopped roasted hazelnuts
50 g/2 oz dark chocolate, melted

1 Mix the ricotta and maple syrup in a bowl. Stir in half the hazelnuts and beat in the melted chocolate.
2 Prepare the baked bananas as in the main recipe.
3 Serve with the ricotta cream and the remaining hazelnuts sprinkled over the top.

Chocolate and Praline Truffle Terrine

A chocolate lover's fantasy – dense, rich and dark! Use a good-quality chocolate with a high content (preferably 50%) of cocoa solids.

375 g/12 oz dark chocolate,
** broken into squares**
2 tablespoons water
175 ml/6 fl oz double cream
75 g/3 oz unsalted butter
1-2 tablespoons rum
75 g/3 oz good-quality candied
** peel (optional)**
PRALINE:
125 g/4 oz sugar
125 g/4 oz whole blanched almonds

1 Grease a 20 x 10 cm/8 x 4 inch loaf tin and line with nonstick baking paper. Oil a baking sheet.

2 To make the praline, combine the sugar and almonds in a small heavy saucepan. Heat gently until the sugar melts, stirring frequently. Continue to cook, stirring occasionally, until the sugar turns a deep golden brown and registers 165°C (330°F) on a sugar thermometer. Immediately remove from the heat and pour the mixture on to the oiled baking sheet, spreading it out slightly. Leave to cool. When the praline is completely cold, crush it into small pieces.

3 Melt the broken chocolate with the measured water in a heatproof bowl over a saucepan of barely simmering water. Remove from the heat and leave to cool slightly.

4 Whip the cream in a bowl until it forms soft peaks. In a separate bowl, cream the butter until soft and fluffy, then slowly stir in the chocolate mixture, followed by the rum. Fold in the cream, crushed praline and the candied peel, if using. Pour the mixture into the lined loaf tin. Level the top, cover and place in the refrigerator for 2-3 hours.

5 To serve, unmould the terrine on to a platter and cut into thin slices. Serve seasonal fresh fruits as an accompaniment.

Serves 6-8
Preparation time: 15 minutes, plus 2-3 hours chilling time

Baked Blueberry Purses with Almond Cream

Plain sugar can be substituted for the vanilla sugar, but the latter is easy to prepare at home. Just steep one or two whole vanilla pods in a jar of sugar – the sugar will be deliciously scented, and you can top up the jar with more sugar as required.

750 g/1½ lb fresh blueberries
6-8 tablespoons vanilla sugar
  (see introduction)
6-8 tablespoons crème de cassis
ALMOND CREAM:
750g/1½ lb ground almonds
1 kg/2 lb mascarpone
3 egg yolks
125 g/4 oz caster sugar
125 ml/4 fl oz double cream
2 tablespoons Amaretto

1 To make the almond cream, first line an 18 cm/7 inch sieve with a piece of muslin large enough to overhang the edge by about 10 cm/4 inches. Place the lined sieve over a bowl.
2 In a mixing bowl, beat the ground almonds with the mascarpone. In a separate bowl, beat the egg yolks with the sugar until pale and fluffy. Fold into the mascarpone mixture.
3 Whip the cream in another bowl until it forms soft peaks. Fold into the mascarpone with the Amaretto. Turn the mixture into the lined sieve, fold the excess muslin over, cover with a small plate and set a small weight on top. Place in the refrigerator for 6-8 hours or overnight, to drain.
4 The blueberries are cooked in individual foil purses. For each purse you will require a 33 x 33 cm/ 13 x 13 inch square of double foil. Heap a quarter of the blueberries in the centre of each foil square and turn up the edges of the foil to form a lip. Sprinkle the blueberries with 1 tablespoon of the vanilla sugar. Drizzle 1 tablespoon of the crème de cassis over the top, bring up the edges of the foil to make a purse and press together to seal.
5 Cook the sealed foil purses on a barbecue grill over moderately hot coals for 8-10 minutes.
6 Unmould the almond cream on to a large plate. Serve portions of the cream beside the blueberries and a jug of single cream, if liked.

Serves 6-8
Preparation time: 15 minutes, plus 6-8 hours draining time (or overnight)
Cooking time: 10 minutes

Grilled Fruit Skewers with Coconut Custard

Serve this rich custard as a rich dipping sauce, rather like a cold fondue. Choose varieties of fruit that will take roughly the same time to cook, and cut them into pieces of uniform size.

1 kg/2 lb assorted fruits in season
  (e.g. mango, papaya, peach,
  strawberries, oranges, apples
  or pears)
lime or lemon juice, for brushing
2 tablespoons muscovado or
  caster sugar

COCONUT CUSTARD:
4 egg yolks
75 g/3 oz caster sugar
150 ml/¼ pint coconut milk
150 ml/¼ pint double cream
1 tablespoon rum, Cointreau or other
  liqueur (optional)

1 To make the coconut custard, first whisk the egg yolks and sugar in a bowl until thick and creamy. Mix the coconut milk and cream in a saucepan. Bring to just below boiling point. Gradually add this hot cream to the beaten egg yolk mixture, whisking constantly, then return to the clean pan. Place the pan over a low heat and stir constantly until the mixture coats the back of a spoon. (Be very careful not to let the mixture boil as this will cause the custard to curdle.) Remove the pan from the heat and immediately strain the custard into a bowl. Stir in the rum or liqueur, if using, and cover the surface closely. When cool, chill the coconut custard in the refrigerator.
2 If using wooden skewers, soak them in cold water for 30 minutes. Prepare the fruit according to type and cut it into evenly sized pieces. Thread on to 8 skewers, alternating the different types of fruit, to create a colourful effect.
3 Brush all the fruit with lime or lemon juice. Cook on a barbecue grill over moderately hot coals for 2-3 minutes on each side, then sprinkle the fruit with the sugar and cook the skewers for 1 minute more.
4 Serve the hot grilled fruit skewers at once, together with a separate bowl of coconut custard for dipping.

Serves 4
Preparation time: 25 minutes, plus 1 hour chilling time
Cooking time: 4-6 minutes

VARIATION

Grilled Fruit Skewers with Rum Butter Glaze

Instead of serving the coconut custard with the fruit skewers, glaze the fruit with this delicious sweetened rum butter.

75 g/3 oz butter
2 tablespoons muscovado sugar
1 tablespoon rum or other liqueur

1 Melt the butter in a small saucepan together with the muscovado sugar. Stir in the rum (or liqueur of your choice) and brush the flavoured butter over the fruit skewers as they cook.

Chestnut Flan with Persimmon Cream Pots

Perfect for autumn – slices of chestnut flan with puréed fruit and cream piled into frozen persimmon shells. The fruit must be very soft and ripe – unripe persimmons have very dry, tannin, unpleasant taste.

500 g/1 lb cooked chestnuts, peeled
125 g/4 oz butter, softened
200 g/7 oz caster sugar
½ teaspoon vanilla essence
2 eggs, separated, plus 1 egg white
1 teaspoon fennel seeds,
    crushed (optional)
icing sugar, for dusting

PERSIMMON POTS:
6 ripe persimmons
350 ml/12 fl oz double cream
3 tablespoons caster sugar
grated nutmeg

1 To prepare the persimmon pots, cut a 5 mm/¼ inch slice off the top of each fruit, making a lid. Using a teaspoon, scoop the persimmon flesh into a sieve set over a bowl, leaving a thin shell. Wrap all the persimmon shells and lids in clingfilm and freeze for 1-2 hours, until firm. Meanwhile, press the persimmon flesh through the sieve, discarding the stones.

2 Purée the chestnuts in a liquidizer or food processor until smooth.

3 Beat the butter, sugar and vanilla essence until light and fluffy. Stir in the egg yolks, chestnut purée and fennel seeds, if using. Mix well.

4 Whisk the egg whites in a grease-free bowl until stiff but not dry. Stir a quarter into the chestnut mixture and gently fold in the rest. Spoon the mixture into a 20 cm/8 inch fluted flan tin. Level the surface. Bake in a preheated oven, 160°C (325°F), Gas Mark 3, for 40-50 minutes, until a skewer inserted in the flan comes out clean. Cool slightly, then transfer to a wire rack and cool completely before serving.

5 Whisk the cream, sugar and nutmeg in a bowl until it forms soft peaks. Fold in the persimmon purée then spoon the mixture into the frozen shells and top with the lids. Dust the flan with icing sugar and serve with the persimmon cream pots.

Serves 6-8
Preparation time: 20 minutes,
plus 1-2 hours freezing time
Cooking time: 40-50 minutes

Champagne Syllabub and Strawberries

What evokes the taste of summer better than perfectly ripened, sweet English strawberries and cream? Here they are served with a velvety Champagne syllabub, ideal for a light but wicked dessert.

150 ml/¼ pint Champagne or dry sparkling wine
2 tablespoons caster sugar
finely grated rind and juice of ½ lemon
300 ml/½ pint double cream
ripe strawberries, to serve

1 Mix the Champagne, sugar, lemon rind and juice together in a large bowl.
2 Add the cream and whisk the mixture until it forms soft peaks.
3 Spoon into glasses and chill for 1-2 hours before serving.
4 Serve with a mixture of cultivated and wild strawberries.

Serves 4
Preparation time: 5-10 minutes, plus 1-2 hours chilling time

Sticky Rice and Ginger in Banana Leaves

Banana leaves are often used in South-east Asia to wrap and protect sweet and savoury food for cooking. Here they provide the packaging for a mixture of sweetened coconut rice and sticky stem ginger. Pieces of exotic fruit can be added instead of, or in addition to, the ginger. Traditionally glutinous rice is used to make sticky rice, but this recipe uses the more readily available short-grain pudding rice.

250 g/8 oz pudding rice
600 ml/1 pint coconut milk
3 tablespoons caster sugar

2 pieces of stem ginger, finely chopped
banana leaves (from ethnic markets)
or foil, for wrapping

1 Rinse the rice in several changes of water until the water runs clear, then drain well. Place the rice in a saucepan with the coconut milk. Bring to the boil, reduce the heat to very low and cover the pan. Simmer gently for about 15-20 minutes, stirring occasionally to prevent sticking, until the rice is tender and the liquid has been completely absorbed.

2 When cooked, transfer the rice to a bowl, stir in the sugar and ginger, cover and set aside to cool slightly.

3 If using the banana leaves, soften them slightly by dipping them in a large saucepan of boiling water. Drain and place on a work surface. Cut the leaves into sixteen 25 x 7 cm/10 x 3 inch strips. Soak several lengths of string in cold water to prevent burning. For each parcel, cross 2 strips of banana leaves on the work surface. Place one eighth of the rice mixture at the centre of each cross and fold over the banana strips to enclose completely. Tie the parcels with the string to secure. Alternatively, make individual parcels with foil.

4 Place the parcels on a barbecue grill over moderately hot coals for 4-5 minutes on each side, until the filling is firm and heated through. Serve hot with exotic fruit.

Serves 4
Preparation time: 15 minutes
Cooking time: 20-25 minutes

Chocolate and Pine Nut Meringue Stack

50 g/2 oz cocoa powder
125 g/4 oz icing sugar
6 egg whites
pinch of salt
175 g/6 oz caster sugar
125 g/4 oz pine nuts, toasted
   and chopped
cocoa powder and icing sugar,
   to decorate

MARSALA CREAM:

2 eggs, separated
2 tablespoons caster sugar
2 tablespoons Marsala
500 g/1 lb mascarpone

1 Line 4 baking sheets with nonstick baking paper. Draw a 20 cm/ 8 inch circle on each.
2 Sift the cocoa powder and icing sugar into a small bowl. Place the egg whites and salt in a separate, grease-free bowl and whisk until stiff but not dry. Gradually whisk in the caster sugar, adding 1 tablespoon at a time. Carefully fold in the sifted icing sugar mixture and chopped pine nuts until evenly combined.
3 Divide the meringue mixture evenly between the circles on the lined baking sheets and spread out evenly with a palette knife. Place the baking sheets in a preheated oven, 150°C (300°F), Gas Mark 2, and bake for 1-1½ hours. Remove from the oven and cool completely on wire racks.
4 To make the Marsala cream, whisk the egg yolks, caster sugar and Marsala in a bowl until creamy, then beat in the mascarpone until well combined. Place the egg whites into a separate, grease-free bowl and whisk until stiff but not dry, then fold them into the mascarpone mixture.
5 Divide the Marsala cream mixture between 3 of the meringue circles, spreading to the edges. Stack the cream-topped meringues on top of each other on a serving plate, then crush the last layer into small pieces and sprinkle on top.
6 Chill the dessert in the refrigerator for 2-4 hours To serve, dust lightly with cocoa powder and icing sugar.

Serves 8-10
Preparation time: 35 minutes
Cooking time: 1½ hours

Rum-flambéed Pineapple Parcels

A simple and simply delicious dessert – and easy to omit the rum from children's portions.

1 ripe pineapple, peeled
50 g/2 oz butter
75 g/3 oz light muscovado sugar
4 tablespoons dark rum
50 g/2 oz pecan nuts, roasted and
**   coarsely chopped**
crème fraîche or fromage blanc to serve

1 Cut the pineapple into 8 even slices, then remove the cores with a small pastry cutter to make rings.
2 Using doubled foil, cut out 4 foil squares, each large enough to hold 2 pineapple rings in a loose parcel. Place 2 rings on each square.
3 Melt the butter in a small pan, stir in the sugar and cook gently until the sugar has dissolved. Divide between the parcels, then bring the edges of the foil together and press to seal.
4 Cook on a grill over moderately hot coals for 10-15 minutes.
5 When the pineapple is cooked, open each package carefully, spoon 1 tablespoon of rum into each and ignite with a match. Scatter over the chopped pecans and serve at once with crème fraîche or fromage blanc.

Serves 4
Preparation time: 15 minutes
Cooking time: 10-15 minutes

Kissel of Summer Berries served with Almond Bread Crisps

A delicious light fruit soup, kissel originated in Eastern Europe. Made with fresh summer berries it would be a stunning and unusual ending to a special occasion barbecue.

1 loaf almond bread (see right)
500 g/1 lb mixed summer berries
    (raspberries, strawberries, cherries
    and red, white or blackcurrants),
    prepared according to type
600 ml/1 pint water

1 tablespoon arrowroot mixed to
    a paste with 2 tablespoons
    water (optional)
3-4 tablespoons sugar
soured cream or fromage blanc, to
    serve (optional)

1 To make the almond bread crisps, cut the loaf into very thin slices and arrange them in a single layer on a baking sheet. Bake the almond bread slices in a preheated oven, 150°C (300°F), Gas Mark 2, for 15-20 minutes, until lightly golden. Cool on wire racks then store in an airtight container.
2 To make the kissel, first set aside 125 g/4 oz of the fruit for decoration. Place the remaining fruit with the measured water in a saucepan. Bring to the boil, then turn off the heat and leave to cool slightly. Pour the contents of the pan into a blender or food processor; process until smooth, then strain through a sieve into a clean saucepan to remove any pips or seeds.
3 Bring the strained fruit purée to the boil. Whisk the arrowroot paste into the purée together with the sugar, to taste. When the purée thickens, pour it into a bowl and cover the surface closely to prevent a skin from forming. Leave to cool, then chill.
4 Pour the chilled kissel into soup plates and decorate with the reserved fruit. Swirl in the soured cream or fromage blanc, if liked, and serve the almond bread crisps separately.

Serves 6
Preparation time: 15 minutes, plus 1 hour chilling time
Cooking time: 15-20 minutes

Almond Bread

The almond bread is best left overnight before slicing so that it will be easier to cut thinly.

2 eggs
125 g/4 oz caster sugar
½ teaspoon vanilla essence
125 g/4 oz plain flour, sifted
125 g/4 oz whole blanched
    almonds, toasted

1 Grease a 20 x 7 cm/8 x 3 inch loaf tin and line it with nonstick baking paper.
2 Whisk the eggs, sugar and vanilla essence in a bowl until thick and creamy and the mixture holds a trail when the whisk is lifted.
3 Carefully fold in the flour and almonds and spoon into the loaf tin. Level the top.
4 Bake the almond bread in a preheated oven, 160°C (325°F), Gas Mark 3, for 30-35 minutes or until a skewer inserted in the loaf comes out clean.
5 Leave to cool slightly in the tin, then invert the almond bread on to a wire rack to cool completely.

Serves 6
Preparation time: 15 minutes
Cooking time: 30-35 minutes